A Better Congress

Change the Rules, Change the Results
A Modest Proposal
A Citizen's Guide to Legislative Reform

By Joseph Gibson

Includes U.S. Constitution and Declaration of Independence

TWO SEAS MEDIA
Alexandria, VA

Rosie the Riveter

"The War Advertising Council's Women in War Jobs campaign is the most successful advertising recruitment campaign in American history. Rosie the Riveter, a fictional character immortalized by posters supporting the war effort and a wartime song of the same name, helped to recruit more than two million women into the workforce.

Her image graced postage stamps and the cover of Smithsonian magazine and before long Rosie the Riveter became a nickname for women working in wartime industries."

Source: "Women in War Jobs—Rosie the Riveter (1942-1945)," Ad Council
<http://www.adcouncil.org/default.aspx?id=128>

"In 1942, Pittsburgh artist J. Howard Miller was hired by the Westinghouse Company's War Production Coordinating Committee to create a series of posters for the war effort. One of these posters became the famous 'We Can Do It!' image—an image that in later years would also become 'Rosie the Riveter,' though not intended at its creation. Miller based his 'We Can Do It!' poster on a United Press photograph taken of Michigan factory worker Geraldine Doyle. Its intent was to help recruit women to join the work force.

At the time of the poster's release the name 'Rosie' was not associated with the image. The poster—one of many in Miller's Westinghouse series—was not initially seen much beyond one Midwest Westinghouse factory where it was displayed for two weeks in February 1942. It was only later, around the 1970s and 1980s, that the Miller poster was rediscovered and became famous as 'Rosie The Riveter.' "

Source: Jack Doyle, "Rosie The Riveter, 1942-1945," PopHistoryDig.com, February 28, 2009. *<http://www.pophistorydig.com/?p=877>*

Cover illustration by Marilyn Gates-Davis

Two Seas Media publications are marketed and distributed by TheCapitol.Net.

Two Seas Media is a non-partisan firm.

Additional copies of *A Better Congress* can be ordered from your favorite bookseller or online: *<www.ABetterCongress.com>*.

Endnotes at *<www.TCNABC.com>*.

Design and production by Zaccarine Design, Inc., Evanston, IL; 847-864-3994.

∞ The paper used in this publication exceeds the requirements of the American National Standard for Information Sciences—Permanence of Paper for Printed Library Materials, ANSI Z39.48-1992.

A Better Congress

Hardbound:	Softcover:	Ebook:
ISBN: 1587332337	ISBN: 158733237X	EISBN: 1587332361
ISBN 13: 978-1-58733-233-3	ISBN 13: 978-1-58733-237-1	EISBN 13: 978-1-58733-236-4

Dedication

To my parents, Lamar Gibson
and the late Betty Gibson,
whose love and tireless efforts
made all things possible for me.

Table of Contents

Part I:
Why Congress Does Not Work Well

Part II:
How to Fix Congress

About the Author

Joseph Gibson has worked in the legislative, executive, and judicial branches of the federal government. He has lobbied members of Congress and their staffs, advocated on behalf of the executive branch, and argued cases in federal and state courts.

He grew up in Waycross, Georgia, and attended Yale University, where he received a bachelor's degree in political science. After graduation, he spent a year working on the staff of the Senate Judiciary Committee. He returned to Yale Law School, where he earned his J.D. degree. After law school, he clerked for the Hon. R. Lanier Anderson, III, of the U.S. Court of Appeals for the Eleventh Circuit in Macon, Georgia. He then returned to Washington, where he spent the next six and a half years as a litigator with private law firms.

He was not particularly interested in politics at the time, but the Republican takeover of Congress in 1994 led, through a series of connections and circumstances, to his getting a job as an antitrust counsel for the House Judiciary Committee. From there, he rose to chief antitrust counsel for the committee. After seven years, he left that job in 2001 and became a deputy assistant attorney general representing the legislative interests of the U.S. Department of Justice.

In 2003, he returned to the committee as its chief legislative counsel and parliamentarian. After two years there, he became chief of staff to Representative Lamar Smith of Texas. When the Republicans lost their majority in the House in the 2006 election, he became chief minority counsel of the committee. He now lobbies on antitrust, intellectual property, and other issues at the law firm of Constantine Cannon LLP in Washington, DC.

He and his wife, Heath, live in Washington and New York with their daughter.

In 2010, TheCapitol.Net published his first book, entitled *Persuading Congress*. That book advises executives how to improve their lobbying strategies.

The views expressed here are entirely his own and do not necessarily represent those of any other person or group.

Preface

Polls regularly reveal profound public dissatisfaction with Congress. Its leaders and its work receive abysmal approval ratings. In one recent poll, a plurality of likely voters declared that 535 people randomly selected from a phone book would perform better than the current Congress.[1] Another found that 75 percent of adults believe that Congress would change for the better if most of its current members were replaced.[2] Still another found that 75 percent of likely voters thought Congress should cut its members' pay until it balances the federal budget.[3]

Generally speaking, it is hard to get 75 percent of people to agree that the sun will rise tomorrow. These extraordinary numbers show something much more intense than run of the mill, everyday complaints about the foibles of politicians.

This deep discontent began in late 2008 with passage of the Troubled Assets Relief Program legislation (TARP). Whatever its actual merits, the public perceived it as bailing out Wall Street at the expense of Main Street. These feelings grew in early 2009 with the passage of a $787 billion stimulus bill. The public questioned that much spending without any obvious economic recovery.

Congress's passage of the 2010 health care reform bill over strong and visible voter opposition continued to stir up these feelings. The lack of popular support was evident during the debate, but Congress passed it anyway. Months after its enactment, polls continue to show that majorities of the public oppose it.[4] In August 2010, 71 percent of Missouri voters voted for a ballot measure intended to invalidate a crucial part of the law.[5] A number of states have sued to overturn the law. The whole episode provides a striking example of an ongoing breakdown of representative government. Despite this growing discontent with Congress, hardly anyone has closely examined why Congress does not work well and suggested realistic ways to change it for the better.

This book starts from the fundamental notion that incentives drive human behavior—a proposition as true for members of Congress as for anyone else. Some of those incentives derive from the basic congressional framework found in Article I of the Constitution. Left alone, these incentives and the constitutional framework function quite well.[6]

The problems with Congress today do not arise from the Constitution. Instead, much of the dysfunction arises from statutes, rules, and practices that Congress has subsequently added to the constitutional structure. Those additions create perverse incentives for members of Congress that produce unpopular results. Over many years, those incentives have collected to the point that they distort the founders' carefully designed original vision of Congress.

Even if we wanted to amend the Constitution to alter the incentives, proposed amendments likely could not clear the constitutional hurdles for ratification.[7] For example, during the 1990s, various groups worked to amend the Constitution to prevent members from serving more than a certain number of terms. Although the idea of term limits was popular, those groups never came close to amending the Constitution.

Part I of this book describes the reasons why Congress does not work well. It examines the incentives that members of Congress face and shows how they combine to undermine the quality of Congress's work. Those incentives form a complex, interrelated web that must be considered as a whole. Its various strands do not necessarily correspond on a one-to-one basis with the solutions that this book offers. Thus, the solutions are set out separately in Part II.

If you want to read about the proposed solutions immediately, skip directly to Part II. It suggests a variety of ways that Congress might change its practices to produce better legislation. Some proposals apply to both chambers; some are specific to the Senate or to the House. Some are more likely to happen than others. Given the current public attitude toward Congress, this is not the time or place for unrealistic, pie-in-the-sky proposals, so this book suggests plausible scenarios that can lead to the enactment of each proposed solution.

On the other hand, this book does not claim that its suggestions are the only possible solutions. It does not try to present an all-inclusive case for its ideas or to rebut every possible counterargument—that would require a much longer and more detailed book. Rather, this book's purpose is to provoke thought—to ignite debate—to imagine other ways of doing things. If its readers conceive even better ideas to improve the workings of Congress, it will have more than served its purpose.

In the 2010 midterms, voters chose a Congress that will act much differently from the one elected in 2008. They clearly wanted to change the results they get from Congress. Following in their wake, this book seeks to inspire Congress to govern itself in new ways that produce better outcomes for the public.

Endnotes

See all endnote links at <www.TCNABC.com>.

1. "41% Say Random Selection From Phone Book Would Do A Better Job Than Current Congress," Rasmussen Reports poll published May 20, 2010.

2. "Dems in power could be in peril, poll says," USA Today/Gallup poll published September 3, 2010.

3. "75% Say Congress Should Cut Its Own Pay Until Budget Is Balanced," Rasmussen Reports poll published, August 31, 2010.

4. Politico/Battleground Poll taken September 19-22, 2010, (42% favorable, 54% unfavorable); CNN/Opinion Research Poll taken August 6-10, 2010 (40% favor, 56% oppose).

5. See Monica Davey, "Missouri Voters Reject Health Law," *The New York Times*, August 3, 2010.

6. For a discussion of the founders' thinking about these incentives, see Federalist Papers Nos. 52-66.

7. U.S. Const., art. V. Constitutional amendments require the concurrence of two-thirds of both chambers of Congress and ratification by three-fourths of the states.

A Better Congress
Change the Rules, Change the Results
A Modest Proposal

A Citizen's Guide to Legislative Reform

Those Who Come to Congress Become Congress

"If you want to get along, go along."
Speaker Sam Rayburn

"When in Rome, do as the Romans do."
St. Ambrose

People always thought that Rick Johnson was somehow different. He was personable, to be sure, but a bit overly ambitious. Back in high school, he wanted to become class president a little too much. It always made one wonder how far he would go to win. He was not a big thinker, but he was an operator. The stories about him were by no means legendary, but everybody had heard them. When the incumbent congresswoman retired, it came as no surprise that Johnson left his successful real estate business to run for Congress.

His wife hesitated because they had two small children. She worried about their family life. Johnson quickly dismissed her concerns. He announced his candidacy in June of the year before the midterm election, which meant seventeen months of campaigning. In Johnson's mind, his wife could run things at home as she always had. His business partner could keep the real estate business going in case Johnson lost.

But Johnson fervently hoped that he would have a new job for life. And he wanted to make a difference—to turn some of his ideas into laws. For example, many of the homes in the district suffered periodically from river flooding. Private insurance companies had long ago realized that that they could not insure these properties and make a

profit. The federal government had stepped into the shoes of the private insurers with the National Flood Insurance Program (NFIP).

With the NFIP, people could go right on building homes along the river even though they were likely to get flooded every few years. Many of the voters in the district used the program. While they found the bureaucracy associated with it maddening, they loved the availability of the insurance that they could not buy in the private market. Johnson wanted to lower their premiums. That would certainly be good for his friends in the real estate business. More importantly, from Johnson's perspective, if he could get his name attached to the idea of lower NFIP premiums, he would hold the seat forever. He would make it a central part of his campaign.

That part was easy. Johnson had thought about the race since he was in college and had always known becoming Mr. Lower Premiums would strengthen him politically. The twelve years he had waited for the incumbent to retire gave him plenty of time to hone his strategy. He knew he had a good plan.

But when his chance finally came, the demands of fund-raising surprised him. Some days during the campaign, all he did was ask for money. Raising $450,000 in increments of $500 and $1,000 required endless phone calls and meetings. He could not believe how much of his time the donors expected for a lousy $250. At least he did not have to run against an incumbent. They usually had a lock on most of the money that was out there. Johnson thanked his lucky stars that his business partner's son, who was just out of college, had agreed to serve as his driver. That let Johnson make calls while they traveled from event to event.

Johnson was also surprised that he did not have to study the issues very much. Reading a couple of newspapers every day was pretty much all he had to do. He knew the NFIP stuff cold from his real estate career, and that affected local people's pocketbooks in a highly visible way. He could always fall back into that when he was at a loss for something to talk about.

Beyond that, the details of the larger national issues really were not his thing. He knew all the important people in the district and how they thought. He could pretty much repeat back to them the platitudes they wanted to hear without breaking a sweat. Because he had never held office before, he had no record to defend. He would get around to revealing what he really wanted to do on other things once he won the election.

Immigration policy was one of those things. The biggest employer in the district processed frozen foods at a facility near the largest town. It had a labor problem. It employed a lot of illegal immigrants. The company's CEO told Johnson that despite the high unemployment in the area, he could not get Americans to take the jobs. When he could get them, they usually did not stay for long and it was expensive to hire new people constantly. If he was going to keep the plant going, he had to hire the illegal immigrants. At least their work supported the higher-paying jobs in the company's headquarters.

Johnson's personal feelings about the issue were mixed. He certainly understood where the CEO was coming from. He also felt great compassion for the illegal immigrants. He had sold many of them their houses, and he knew that they were good, hard-working people. Many of them could only buy those houses because of NFIP, so he knew that his idea on that was a winner with their community.

But the majority of citizens in the district resented their employment at the plant even while the citizens often employed the very same people for odd jobs. For that reason, he could never support a citizenship bill along the lines of what the groups representing the illegal immigrants wanted. He would have to figure out a way to dance around the issue. Perhaps with a meaningless gesture here and some double-talk there, he would keep all of them happy. And if that did not work, he hoped at least to keep them from being mad at him.

While Johnson was plotting his steps through the immigration mine field, he got some great news. The one candidate who might have beaten him decided not to run. Sheila Wilkinson, an innovative architect and successful community leader, had won numerous professional and community service awards and was widely admired. Beating her

would have tested all of Johnson's skills. She had devised some innovative ways of minimizing flood damage to houses. People had started to use them widely and they had saved money as a result. Many of them appreciated Wilkinson's contributions in that area.

She had also started a charity that encouraged people not to rebuild homes in the flood-prone areas. Through this group, she had helped a number of the illegal immigrants to get into better housing. She had shown them some ways to build cheaper housing in other areas. That prevented them from having to go through the misery of the floods every few years. The group had also helped a number of them pursue their legal rights under immigration law. Because of these efforts, she had a street credibility that Johnson could not match.

But Wilkinson had a big weakness—she frequently said what she actually thought. She also did not keep doing the same thing over and over and expecting a different result. For example, she thought that the NFIP was an insane government program. She did not mind saying that she would work to eliminate it if she were in Congress. Subsidizing people to rebuild homes in flood plains made no sense regardless of how good it might have been for her business. If the private insurers could not turn a profit writing that insurance, the government should encourage people to put the land to better use—not to build houses there. For Wilkinson, it was as simple as that.

On immigration, Wilkinson thought the entire debate in Congress missed the point. From her experience working with the illegal immigrants, she believed that most of them would have preferred to live in their home countries if they could have made any kind of decent living there. When the frozen food plant had cut jobs during the recession, many of the illegal immigrants who lost their jobs had headed home. Life here without a job was no better than life at home. Rather than debating amnesty and fences, she thought Congress ought to try to exert leverage on the home countries to improve conditions there. Ultimately, that would give the illegal immigrants the incentive to return home to a better life.

Privately, Johnson thought that what Wilkinson said made a lot of sense. Had she run, however, he felt confident that he could have used her statements on both issues to defeat her. For a variety of reasons, he was glad that he would not have to.

After a lot of thought, Wilkinson decided that she could do more good in her current role than she could in Congress. She had three small children and did not want to leave them to campaign or to live in Washington. She did not want to spend two years of her life asking for money. She could have partially funded the race herself, but if she lost, that money would be gone forever. She did not want to spend time fighting with the purists in her party about her unorthodox views.

She knew that if she were honest and said what she really thought about NFIP and immigration, she would probably lose to Johnson. But for her, if she had to fake who she was, it just was not worth it. She also knew that to have any chance of getting things done in Congress, she would have to be there for years. It was definitely not what she wanted to do for the rest of her life. She loved architecture too much.

She concluded that she could probably do more about flooding by continuing to come up with better ways to build houses. She could probably do more for the illegal immigrants by keeping her charity going. In the end, her decision was easy. She had one full-time job—she did not need another one.

Had it been more of a part-time thing like the charity, she might have done it. The state legislature worked that way. Her business partner had won a seat there, and she had been able to make the part-time arrangement work. Wilkinson wished Congress worked differently, but as always, she operated in the world of reality, not wishful thinking.

Once Wilkinson was out of the way, the path was clear for Johnson. After months of campaigning, he won the crowded primary. His ecstatic friends and supporters celebrated on the night of the primary. At the victory party, Johnson felt elated, but his wife had a dull, empty feeling in the pit of her stomach. It was the first time Johnson had seen her and the kids for two and a half weeks. She suspected that their life had changed forever.

The day after the primary, Johnson caught up with them between

the numerous meetings and phone calls he had to make right away. He wished he had more time to spend with them, but his political dreams needed his attention. He breathed deeply and plunged back into a new round of campaigning and fund-raising. After several more months on the campaign merry-go-round, he won the general election.

At last he was on his way to Washington! Johnson could hardly wait. His wife decided that she and the kids would live at home and see him on the weekends. That disappointed him, but finally winning his seat in Congress more than overcame it.

His arrival in Washington only confirmed that he had made the right decision. All his life, he had felt that people never quite gave him the respect he deserved. That changed on his first day in the Capitol. Everyone he saw seemed to know him already. And they could not have treated him better if he had been a visiting head of state. All the women were friendly—a pleasant new experience. Johnson thought to himself that this was going to be even better than he had envisioned.

In spite of the good feelings, his first meeting with his party's leader knocked him for a loop. The old guy told him to keep his nose clean, his mouth shut, and his hand out. Their party needed to raise a lot of money if it was ever going to win the majority back. The party expected him to contribute to that effort and to vote the party line. The old guy then informed him that he would get his third choice of committees— Small Business. The old guy said that would be a good fit for him since he had owned a small real estate agency. Besides, he had a safe seat, and the party needed to give its seats on the good fund-raising committees to the members who had marginal districts. That left Johnson without a seat on Financial Services, where had hoped to establish his NFIP bona fides.

Johnson's disenchantment deepened when he actually got to a Small Business Committee hearing. The chair of the committee recognized him to speak only after all the other members had taken their turns. By that time, the audience had dwindled to almost nothing, and the witnesses barely paid him any attention. Not that many people came to Small Business Committee hearings anyway.

When the committee met to vote on bills, it was much the same. The first three times he thought about offering an amendment, the committee's minority staff discouraged him from doing so. They and their boss, the ranking member, did not want Johnson to do anything that might make the bills better.

Granted, Johnson had not spent a lot of time pondering the amendments. He had simply told his staff to crib from the position papers that some interest groups had sent him. Then they drafted some similar amendments. Nonetheless, Johnson thought that they were pretty good. At a minimum, they would give him a moment in the sun. It was not to be. From his perspective, the committee staff had more influence than he did. They seemed to make the decisions on how the markups went. All he did was vote.

Occasionally, the other party proposed some reasonable ideas. He even considered voting for a couple of them. But when word of that got back to the committee's ranking member, he looked at Johnson like he was from another planet. The ranking member asked Johnson if he wanted to get the majority back or not. Johnson followed the ranking member's lead, but he began to wonder what he was supposed to be doing here—other than raising money, of course.

Soon his chief of staff—his partner's son, the driver during the campaign—brought him even worse news. The other party had recruited a strong candidate to challenge him in the next election. To compete effectively, Johnson would have to start raising some serious money.

The chief of staff strongly suggested that Johnson hire a professional fund-raising firm and begin holding events with Washington lobbyists. Johnson balked at first, but after doing a couple of dinners, he came to like them. The lobbyists always treated him with the respect he thought a member of Congress deserved. And they listened to his policy ideas with a rapt attention that more senior members never gave him.

Before long, he was spending almost all of his free time going to fund-raisers. Some were his own fund-raisers and the rest were those

of his friends in Congress. After he began his fund-raising push, he had almost no time to think about the bills he voted on every day.

It was not long before the lobbyists he met began to ask him to cosponsor bills. For the most part, that was easy. For example, he had become good friends with the guy who represented the frozen food processor in his district. One day as they left a fund-raising lunch together, the guy asked Johnson to sign on to a resolution recognizing "National Frozen Food Week." Johnson laughed and said, sure. They were alone, so he asked the guy why they bothered with this kind of meaningless stuff. The guy said, "Hey, it gives us something to put in the newsletter. It makes the CEO think we accomplished something." A little light went off in Johnson's head. Pretty soon, he became a serial cosponsor.

By this time, whenever he planned to speak in committee or on the floor, he just got his party's talking points from his staff and repeated them at the appropriate moments. The parrot act did not bother him that much. Johnson had realized that if you were not a chair or a ranking member, you did not need to waste your time on policy. The committee staff members would probably decide everything anyway.

He knew he was not going to get to do anything meaningful on NFIP until he could work his way on to the Financial Services Committee. That was going to be at least two or three Congresses. In the meantime, he made the most of the tools he had. He introduced a bill that embodied his idea to lower premiums. He talked about it every chance he got, but never mentioned that it was not going anywhere. It might not make it into law, but if he kept talking it up enough, it could make him into Mr. Lower Premiums.

It was all very frustrating, but Johnson decided you might as well spend your time doing something to help yourself win reelection. The NFIP bill was one way to do that. That focus became his saving grace. Despite the emptiness of his efforts in the policy arena, Johnson found fulfillment in competing against the other party politically. He never even thought of not running for a second term—it just never crossed his mind. Washington life had seduced him after only a year. Yes, his family life was suffering because of his long absences, but he would never voluntarily return to selling real estate.[1] Too many people on the other side of the table did not need him there. But in Washington, many people he met hung on his every word. He found it intoxicating.

Plus, the whole system favored incumbents. He would have to get out and work, but his challenger, though a strong one, would struggle mightily to overcome all the advantages he now had as a sitting member. Everyone in the district knew his name; the taxpayers paid for his government staff, and the Washington lobbyists willingly funded his campaign. All they really asked was that he cosponsor a bill or sign a letter to the administration every now and then. That was easy and free. At the same time, his challenger would have to start from scratch—just as Johnson had done two years before. Just let him try, Johnson laughed to himself. It was good to be an incumbent.

Johnson would have to go through the motions, but knew he would win his own race. That knowledge allowed him to spend a lot of time helping his party try to win some of the more marginal seats that might bring them back into the majority. That in turn would get him some credit with his party's leaders and allow him to move up in the next Congress. If he raised enough, he might even get on to the Financial Services Committee next time.

Rick Johnson and Sheila Wilkinson are fictions, but their stories are typical. Notably absent from Johnson's story is any incentive for him to work with members of the other party to develop wise policies. Indeed, he had little time or incentive to think about policy. Johnson came to Congress with a serious, though self-interested, desire to make a difference. Before he had even gotten his seat warm, the incentives that drive members had pushed him into an endless campaign to defeat the other party. Let's see how that happens.

Endnotes

See all endnote links at <www.TCNABC.com>.

1. For more on members' family lives, see Michael L. Koempel and Judy Schneider, *Congressional Deskbook: The Practical and Comprehensive Guide to Congress*, § 1.60 Family Life (5th ed. 2007) (hereafter *Congressional Deskbook*).

Part I

Why Congress Does Not Work Well

Chapters 1–9

Chapter One

The Fortress of Incumbency

"Safety does not happen by accident."
Unknown

"Competition is the whetstone of talent."
Traditional Proverb

Having read this far, you might ask why voters simply don't replace the incumbents if they are so dissatisfied with them? A recent poll found that 55 percent of likely voters thought that incumbents get reelected not because they do a good job, but because they have rigged the rules in their favor.[1] And though he would never say it publicly, our fictional Rick Johnson definitely felt that way. His patient twelve-year wait for the incumbent to retire propelled his campaign. Had he risked a challenge to the incumbent in earlier years, he likely would have lost.

Having won his congressional seat, Rick Johnson saw it as a mighty fortress. Safely ensconced within it, he faced little threat to his position. His primary concern was not how to keep the seat, but how to use it to build his influence in future Congresses.

The 2010 midterm election vividly illustrates this point. Experts rated it extraordinarily competitive because 10–12 Senate seats and 80–100 House seats were "in play"—they could potentially switch from one party's control to the other's. But 37 (out of 100) Senate seats and all 435 House seats were on the ballot. In one of the most hotly contested elections in years, the outcome was seriously in doubt for only about a tenth of the Senate's seats and about a fifth of the House's seats. To put it another way, in 2010, 90 percent of senators and 80 percent of representatives had no realistic fear that they might lose their jobs.[2] In

a more typical year, the parties seriously contest even fewer seats and even more incumbents retain their seats.

These figures provide our first clue about why Congress does not work well: most congressional elections are not competitive. Most incumbents rarely face a serious competitor—even in a bad year for their party. As their congressional careers continue, most incumbents tend to become politically stronger and less vulnerable to defeat so long as they avoid scandals. The whetstone of competition rarely sharpens their talent.

Incumbents begin a campaign with numerous competitive advantages. Some are natural and, to some extent, unavoidable. Others exist because, over the years, incumbents have set up the rules to help themselves get reelected most of the time.

Simply by having run and gotten elected, incumbents achieve some name recognition in their districts. During the decade of 2000–2010, most House members represented approximately 700,000 people. Senators from large states represented millions.[3] With those kinds of numbers, most of their constituents will never meet their congressional representatives or know much about them.

If they do, the constituent will probably associate the member with his party and perhaps with a particular issue (remember Rick Johnson's desire to make himself Mr. Lower Premiums). Given their lack of personal knowledge, a significant portion of voters simply choose a name they have heard before or a party label because they have little or no other information about the candidates. Johnson worked hard to ensure that when people recalled his name, they also recalled lower premiums. That is about as far as members get with most voters. Barring unusual circumstances, an incumbent will likely get most of those name-recognition votes. This tendency also explains why former members as well as spouses, children, or others with the same last name as recent incumbents may also have an advantage at the ballot box.

Having won his first election, a member has many ways to build on that initial name recognition. The member immediately receives a wide variety of resources that the taxpayers fund: a steady paycheck; staff of various sorts; office space; a web site; money to fund mailings, town halls, constituent case work, and other outreach activities; money to fund various types of travel; research services; venues and equipment that make it easy to talk with the media; access to executive branch officials; and many more.[4] As members gain seniority within Congress, their access to these public resources tends to increase.

Members no doubt legitimately need some portion of these resources to represent constituents adequately. But the resources have grown steadily over the years to become a tremendous advantage for incumbents. Congress does have rules that prevent their use for explicit political purposes. However, a skilled politician can stay well within those rules and still use the resources to build his name recognition and burnish his image.

But that is not all. The newly minted incumbent also taps into the national apparatus of his political party. The national party does many things to win a majority in each chamber of Congress in the next election. In doing so, it almost always supports incumbents and provides them with many services. These may include: political advice, access to funds other members have contributed, access to other donors, joint fund-raising activities, advertising campaigns, and speaking opportunities.

At the same time, the national party almost always discourages challenges to incumbents from within the party. Potential challengers who want a political career can earn the long-term scorn of their party if they do not heed its admonitions to stay away from congressional incumbents. That "party scorn" can derail any future races that the potential candidate may be eyeing.

Organized interest groups also take an interest in the new member.[5] These groups have a finite amount of money to donate to candidates. They get the most influence per dollar if they give to winners. Because the winners are almost always incumbents, they direct most of their campaign contributions to incumbents. In some cases, they may also fear retaliation if they do not give to an incumbent.[6]

To lessen the influence of organized interests, campaign finance law limits the contributions that their political arms (known as political action committees or PACs) can give to a candidate to $5,000 per election.[7] This limit produces a number of perverse effects. The important one for purposes of this chapter is that it protects incumbents.[8]

This protection occurs in several ways. According to OpenSecrets.org, the average cost of a winning campaign for a House seat in 2008 was $1.1 million. For a Senate seat, the comparable figure in 2008 was $6.5 million.[9] With a maximum contribution of $5,000, any candidate must receive many contributions to amass a total war chest approaching these numbers.[10]

For many reasons, an incumbent usually has a much larger network of potential donors to draw on than a challenger does. Most incumbents run a more or less permanent campaign, and they are usually perceived as the likely winner. Thus, they often begin with money in the bank, start raising money earlier, and can convince contributors to give sooner than challengers can. Because they have many favors to dispense, they can create specific reasons for donors to give much more often than challengers can.

Finally, most organized interests sit in Washington. Thus, an incumbent can more easily reach them to ask for donations. He may also meet more of them through the process of lobbying, and they are more likely to know him because he is more visible as a sitting member. The contribution limit also forces the organized interests to spread the same amount of money over a larger number of incumbents.

But the contribution limit works to protect incumbents in a different way. It prevents a few significant contributors from bankrolling the campaign of their preferred challenger. Suppose, for example, that the frozen food processor wanted to replace Johnson with Sheila Wilkinson. Under current law, the CEO would have to get a lot of other people to help him. The circle of those brave enough to take on the incumbent must be much larger than it would be absent the limit.

Aside from contribution limits, compliance with the many other arcane aspects of campaign finance law requires significant legal and accounting help. That takes money. The challenger's costs may roughly equal the incumbent's, but because the challenger generally has less cash these costs leave him with fewer resources to get his message out. The incumbent will generally already have the expertise in hand while a challenger must spend time to find it. For all these reasons, the campaign finance laws form one of the strongest pillars of the fortress of incumbency.

Beyond money, holding a seat in Congress gives the member a megaphone that a challenger cannot hope to equal. He has many opportunities to communicate with voters through his normal representational duties, such as constituent mail, an official web site, newsletters, and C-Span coverage of official proceedings. He has ready access to the local and national press. The press often treats his actions as inherently newsworthy because he holds office. For the same reason, he gets invited to events that are newsworthy but not necessarily political—store openings, graduations, and the like. Over time, he builds relationships with reporters that may lead to favorable coverage and to access to non-public information. All of these factors may give him an advantage in the competition for press endorsements as well. A challenger has few or none of these.

An incumbent might argue that this press access is both a blessing and a curse. For example, incumbents face more scrutiny of their behavior than a challenger would. Publicly reported scandals destroy more incumbent fortresses than any other factor. But even in this arena, the rules favor incumbents. Both chambers have processes to address member misconduct.[11] However, those processes take interminable amounts of time to come to a conclusion. If members do not suffer a criminal conviction, their chamber's ethics procedure rarely punishes them seriously. Negative press coverage of a scandal usually damages the member much more than the actual ethics process.

All of the reasons discussed so far give any incumbent a leg up over any challenger. In many districts, the incumbent has additional advantages if the challenger represents the other major party. Many districts lean strongly to one major party or the other. Absent a scan-

dal or some other unusual circumstance, that party almost always renominates its incumbent. When that incumbent nominee reaches the general election, he generally coasts to victory.[12]

Third party or independent challengers face even greater impediments. Under the Constitution, the state legislatures set the rules for congressional elections.[13] In most instances, they have chosen a first-past-the-post system, meaning that whoever gets the most votes wins. Moreover, our system uses binary, winner-take-all elections without any provision for proportional representation for minority parties. These two features of our system strongly encourage a two-party system. Thus, only in rare instances do third parties have an infrastructure approaching that of the Democratic and Republican parties. In most states, any independent challenger must expend a great deal of time and effort just to get his name on the ballot. For the official Democratic and Republican nominees, ballot access is usually more or less automatic.[14]

In most instances, winning a seat in Congress provides the incumbent with a mighty political fortress. Those who would storm it and throw the incumbent out face a Herculean task. Because most incumbents are so safe, they become comfortable in the job and begin to think that they are not vulnerable to defeat. As the Roman poet Ovid put it: "A horse never runs so fast as when he has other horses to catch up [to] and outpace." With no other horses to catch, the typical incumbent feels little inspiration to run faster. At the same time, he may begin to feel that he can to some extent ignore the wishes of their constituents. Much of Congress's mischief arises from that lack of competition.

Endnotes

See all endnote links at <www.TCNABC.com>.

1. "Fairness of Elections: 55% Say Most in Congress Reelected Because the Rules Are Rigged," Rasmussen Reports poll published September 21, 2010.

2. For this reason, predicting many election results is less of a challenge than it appears at first blush.

3. This book refers to both senators and representatives generically as "members" unless there is a need to distinguish between the two. Likewise, it refers to both congressional districts and states as "districts" unless there is a need to distin-

guish between them. Finally, this book uses the masculine pronouns "he" or "him" in referring to members for convenience.

4. For more on these resources generally, see *Congressional Deskbook*, Chapter 5, "Supporting Congress: Allowances and Staff." For more on constituent outreach activities, see *Congressional Deskbook*, § 3.10 Constituency Pressure.

5. This book uses the term "organized interests" rather than "special interests." So-called "special interests" are not special. They are simply groups of citizens trying to get their way in the legislative process. They are neither worse nor better than other citizens. What distinguishes them is that they have organized a united effort to accomplish their goals. For more on the nature of organized interest groups, see Joseph Gibson, *Persuading Congress*, Chapter 12, "Interest Groups and Lobbyists" (2010) (hereafter *Persuading Congress*) and Deanna Gelak, *Lobbying and Advocacy*, § 1.4 What Are Special Interests? (2008) (hereafter *Lobbying and Advocacy*).

6. For more on how organized interests can contribute to congressional campaigns, see *Lobbying and Advocacy*, §§ 2.25, 2.26, 2.27, and 2.28 (political campaigns and compliance).

7. In 2010, campaign contributions from individuals were limited to $2,400 per election as well. For purposes of these restrictions, primaries and general elections are treated as separate elections. For more on compliance with election laws, see the web site of the Federal Election Commission, "Help with Reporting and Compliance," at: *<http://fec.gov/info/compliance.shtml>* and *Congressional Deskbook*, §§ 2.10, 2.20.

8. The individual limitation has the same effect as the limitation on PAC contributions. This book generally refers only to the PAC limitation to simplify the discussion. See "Quick Answers to PAC Questions" from the FEC.

9. "Money Wins Presidency and 9 of 10 Congressional Races in Priciest U.S. Election Ever," OpenSecretsBlog, November 5, 2008.

10. For more on the financial pressures of congressional campaigns, see *Lobbying and Advocacy*, § 2.25 The Financial Pressures of Political Campaigns.

11. For more on congressional ethics, see *Congressional Deskbook*, § 4.30.

12. Occasionally, an incumbent representative will lose because the state legislature redraws his district unfavorably after a census. An incumbent senator or representative may also lose because evolving demographics change his district's partisan leaning. But both of these situations are very much the exception rather than the rule.

13. U.S. Const., art. I, sec. 4.

14. In 2010, several Senate candidates who unexpectedly lost primaries contemplated write-in campaigns in the general election. Only one, Senator Lisa Murkowski of Alaska, actually launched such an effort. For more information about write-in candidates, see the Wikipedia article: "Write-in candidate" and *<www.YouCanWriteIn.com>*.

Chapter Two

The Ordeals of a Campaign

"An election is a moral horror, as bad as a battle except for the blood; a mud bath for every soul concerned in it."

George Bernard Shaw

"The hardest thing about any political campaign is how to win without proving that you are unworthy of winning."

Adlai Stevenson

Running a credible campaign for Congress requires resources that are far beyond the reach of most Americans.[1] Thus, we start with a relatively narrow pool of people who can even conceivably mount a campaign. The people who have the resources tend to be those who already have comfortable lives.

Remember that our fictional Rick Johnson benefited greatly from his strongest potential opponent's decision not to run. If Sheila Wilkinson had taken the plunge, he might never have made it to Washington. Although she might have made a better member of Congress, she concluded that her private life was too valuable and the cost of running was too high. Against that backdrop, look at the decision that a potential candidate faces when deciding whether to run.[2]

If he contemplates running against a sitting member, the upstart confronts all the defenses of the incumbent fortress. His opponent likely already has lots of money in the bank and a political operation in place. The challenger has none of that. If the incumbent comes from his own party, the challenger's fellow partisans will probably treat his candidacy with disdain and derision. If he runs on the minority party ticket

in a partisan district, experts will opine that he has little chance of winning. All of that comes before he gets to the logistics of the campaign itself.

To run a congressional campaign, the potential candidate must be ready to devote himself to campaigning full time for anywhere from a year to two years depending on the local circumstances. Relatively few Americans can leave their livelihoods for that amount of time.[3] Even if they can, it requires a significant sacrifice. If the prospective candidate owns a business, he will likely need to turn it over to his co-owners or subordinates. If he has a professional practice, he must leave it to his partners. His partners and his clients may or may not be there if he returns after a losing campaign. If he is an employee, either he must have an unusually understanding employer or he must leave his job with no promise of one in the future. In the course of a campaign, he may need to say things that offend his potential customers or employers. None of this will help his future livelihood.

Throughout the one- or two-year period of the campaign, he will have to travel to political events constantly. The rigors of bad food, little sleep, and constant separation will wreak physical and emotional havoc on him and his family. The inevitable emotional ups and downs will not make the campaign easier.

He will need to spend much of his time raising money. As noted in Chapter 1, not only must he raise a lot of money, but because of the campaign contribution limits, he must raise it from many different people. That takes time, money, persuasive skills, and a big network of friends. He will endure constant disappointment when people whom he thought were his friends turn him down again and again. Like Rick Johnson, the amount of his time that people will feel entitled to in return for paltry contributions will frustrate him. To become credible, he will have to raise this money relatively early on. If he is wealthy, he has the option of funding his own campaign in whole or in part, but that places a large financial burden on him.

When he is not raising money, he must master skills that he may not have had before. He must learn his district and what its voters care about. Unlike Rick Johnson, not all first-time candidates have studied their districts or planned their campaigns for years. He must meet and greet thousands of voters and show empathy for their concerns. He must become informed about a wide variety of issues and be able to speak intelligently about them at a moment's notice. He must give public speeches. He must deal with the press. He must learn to use any number of modern communications tools—web sites, YouTube, Facebook, Twitter, and all the rest.[4]

The potential candidate must also throw his entire personal life open to press scrutiny. If he has any skeletons in his closet, they will almost certainly come clattering out of it during the course of the campaign. If he has any disgruntled former employees or lovers, they will inevitably emerge to tell tales about him. If his business dealings have been less than circumspect, that too will come out. If there are embarrassing pictures taken in college, they will likely surface. If he has ever said anything dumb in public, the tape will show up on the Internet for all to view. If he has hidden anything, it will come out.

After overcoming all of these obstacles and mounting a campaign, the odds suggest that he will lose. He then returns to his previous life. He may find his livelihood damaged and his reputation besmirched. He has little to show for his troubles other than having seen his name in the newspapers a few times. Worse yet, those mentions likely did not flatter him. All in all, the rigors of a congressional campaign are not enticing.

As noted at the outset, the people who have the resources to even think seriously about running for Congress comprise a small subset of the total population. Many within that subset will find themselves effectively disqualified for one reason or another. These factors can range from belonging to the wrong party to having not lived in the district long enough to having gotten in trouble with the law. All sorts of things narrow the pool further.

Now let's look at those people remaining in the pool. Most of them look like Sheila Wilkinson. They are earning a good living. They are usually well-respected in their communities. Their spouse may have no

interest in entering political life. They have children to raise and educate, and they have the income to do that. They have a vacation home and they go there whenever they can. They lead generally happy lives even if the political bug has bitten them.

They take a look at the ordeal of a campaign. Like Wilkinson, they decide that they do not need the hassle. They would like to serve in Congress, but they do not want to do what it takes to get this job. The prize glitters before them, but they conclude it is not worth the cost and the struggle. Like Wilkinson, they believe that they can do more good where they are.

For all the reasons discussed above, current campaign requirements work to protect incumbents. They discourage worthy candidates from running. If campaigns were easier and more attractive to run, we would have more candidates and more competitive elections. If voters had more choices, that might lead to better results.

Undoubtedly, congressional campaigns severely test those candidates who do run. But the real question is whether they test for the skills needed to make wise policy. We turn to that question in the next chapter.

Endnotes

See all endnote links at <www.TCNABC.com>.

1. For more on congressional campaigns, see *Congressional Deskbook*, § 2.10 Campaigns and Elections.

2. For more on the kinds of people who run for Congress, see *Persuading Congress*, Chapter 3, "Members of Congress."

3. Campaign finance law does allow a campaign to pay a salary to a candidate, but this is rarely done because of the appearance and, more practically, the lack of money.

4. For more on how candidates can use these tools, see *Media Relations Handbook*, by Brad Fitch, Chapter 6, "Web-Based and Online Communications" (2004).

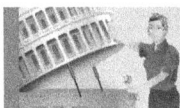

Chapter Three

The Skills Mismatch

*"The qualities that get a man into power
are not those that lead him, once established,
to use power wisely."*

Lyman Bryson
American Educator and Media Adviser

"You campaign in poetry. You govern in prose."

Mario Cuomo

f we could somehow identify perfect legislators outside the context of elections, what qualities would we want in them? Wisdom, judgment, fairness, knowledge, thoughtfulness, modesty, reflection, attention to detail, decisiveness, public-spiritedness? In a hypothetical utopian Congress, legislators with these qualities would enact better policy. But this list would probably not lead us to select our fictional Rick Johnson to serve. He comes across as somewhat lacking when measured against it.

Unfortunately, however, we must choose our legislators in the real world and under current rules. Despite the difficulties of campaigning under those rules, no congressional seat has ever gone vacant because no one chose to run for it. Somebody runs and wins every time. The incentives embedded in those rules do not necessarily operate to select the qualities we might want. But they do attract and reward certain types of candidates—candidates like Rick Johnson. Those candidates have a set of skills that allows them to earn their seats in Congress.

What sets them apart? Most importantly, the winning candidate must decide to run. When a prospective candidate considers a campaign, he must mull over all the factors discussed in Chapters 1 and 2.

And then he must still decide to run. That alone takes a person who is unusually ambitious and self-confident. When the voice in their head says "No. Don't do it. It's not worth it," most people say to themselves: "You know, you're right. What was I thinking?" But those who get to Congress say something else: "It is worth it, and I can do it."

Having decided to run, what other skills and resources does a candidate need to win? The ability to persuade comes first. He must convince a large number of people to donate money to his campaign and to vote for him. Without those essential elements, his campaign will go nowhere. In most cases, he will not know in advance which people will answer yes. Thus, he must ask for money and votes over and over. Much more often than not, people will turn him down. Getting no for an answer must not deter him in the least. Day after discouraging day, he must persist single-mindedly in pursuing his campaign.

To raise the requisite amount of money, it helps to start with a large network of friends. Most candidates begin with some sort of base, but it is absolutely necessary to grow a larger network in the course of the campaign. Because the available time is finite, the candidate must meet people briefly, make a good impression on them, and get them to commit to him. The best candidates will excel at short, but pleasant encounters with large numbers of people. Because he will spend so much time away from his family, the candidate will do better if he can fulfill some of his need for human interaction in these kinds of encounters. Someone who yearns for something deeper will not thrive in this environment.

Short, but pleasant might also describe the best candidates' encounters with the issues. Congress addresses a vast number of them, and, taken as a whole, they are more than any one person can master. A good candidate learns a safe line or two that he can say about each of the most pertinent issues when the need arises. He rarely has time to study them more fully unless they are likely to decide the campaign. If he can formulate his lines in a way that most people can understand, then he is even better off. But a person who feels uncomfortable talking about issues without knowing them in depth will constantly feel ill-at-ease running for Congress. The need to be a mile wide and an inch deep will likely frustrate such a person.

The congressional candidate cannot be a wallflower. He must also find ways to draw attention to himself. Campaigns and elections turn most voters off. They have little interest in what candidates have to say. Successful candidates find ways to make otherwise mundane matters interesting. That gets them in the news and builds their all-important name recognition.

This need for flashiness also affects the candidate's consideration of policy. He will want to talk about policy in a way that interests the public regardless of the policy's underlying wisdom. That is why Rick Johnson wanted to be Mr. Lower Premiums. In his own mind, he knew quite well that his idea would subsidize rebuilding in flood plains. But he also knew that the idea would grab the attention of the voters who wanted to do it. He needed to get noticed by voters, not Washington policy wonks. By the same token, had Sheila Wilkinson run and advocated getting rid of the program, she would have gotten kudos from some think tanks, but derisive jeers from the voters whose wealth was tied up in houses built in reliance on the program.

Ultimately, a congressional election turns on popularity. A successful candidate must develop the ability to say things that appeal to voters based on the current state of public opinion. Public opinion shifts frequently and candidates must shift with it.

That does not mean that candidates do not take their beliefs seriously. Quite the contrary, in most cases, the candidate's deeply held beliefs provided the initial spark to run. But candidates also want to win. They find ways to state their beliefs that allow members of their audience to hear what they want to hear. That is what Rick Johnson tried to do on immigration. He chose to emphasize different aspects of the issue depending on the exigencies of the moment and the preferences of the audience.

Rare indeed is the candidate who has the backbone to talk about wise policy at the expense of popularity. It simply does not pay to do so. Running for Congress is hard and it is all-consuming. Having taken

on the task, candidates do what it takes to win. Sheila Wilkinson did not run in part because she did not want to run as someone other than herself.

If that is where the current rules drive candidates, where does it leave the public at large? Sadly, the skills needed to win do not necessarily lead to wise policymaking. In fact, some of them undermine it.

As we have discussed, to suffer the slings and arrows of a congressional campaign, a candidate must have a thick skin. That is well and good, but this thick skin also tends to include overconfidence in the member's own judgments. Having taken on a congressional campaign and won despite numerous naysayers, a member may begin to believe that his judgment about political matters exceeds that of others. This natural human reaction tends to grow over time as a member wins more elections. When the time comes to decide on policy, it can cause a member to rely solely on his own judgment rather than relying on a wide variety of inputs.

And congressional campaigns tend to favor those who make snap judgments rather than those who think deeply. Although campaigns take a long time, they tend to run at an unnerving, helter-skelter pace. That pace rewards those who think quickly and do not dawdle over their decisions. For campaign purposes, this works well, but wise policy usually requires more reflection. Successful candidates usually have developed a tendency to judge policy without thinking about it in depth. That is what campaigns require, and candidates tend to carry that tendency into government.

Having won a seat in Congress, members must constantly build name recognition if they want to stay in office. To keep their permanent campaigns going, they must keep their name in the news. This need encourages them to advocate policies and actions based on what will get news coverage rather than what will help the country. Rick Johnson talked about improving NFIP every chance he got. That is what voters and the press in his district cared about. If he thought privately that getting rid of NFIP was the best policy, he was never going to say it. Even if he had been willing to say why he thought getting rid of NFIP was the best policy, he could not explain the reasons why in a hundred words or less. And everyone would have thought he was taking something away from them.

Good policy can often be difficult to devise and boring to explain. Doing nothing may make the member look like he does not care about a problem. The press does not want to cover policy proposals that are not exciting. They want copy that will sell advertising. If members want press coverage, they must make their proposals newsworthy, not necessarily wise. That sustains their long-term political survival.[1]

Finally, most members' desire for reelection chills any inclination they may have to pursue wise but unpopular policies. Congress's inability to deal with the financial mess it has created in the major entitlement programs represents the classic case of this phenomenon. Everyone knows that these programs cannot continue indefinitely in their current forms, but few members are willing to take the political heat for pushing the needed reforms.

In short, the skills needed to win a seat in Congress differ significantly from those needed to make wise policy. This is not to say that members do not have good policymaking skills—many of them do. It is just that when that occurs, it is often happenstance. The current campaign rules do not operate to produce members with great legislative ability. Rather, members bring legislative ability to Congress in spite of what they had to do to win their seats. Beyond that, most members' reelection efforts further inhibit them from making wise policy and worsen the problem. When a new member comes to Washington, he enters an environment that further encourages all the worst tendencies of campaigning. We now turn to the specifics of that environment.

Endnotes

See all endnote links at <www.TCNABC.com>.

    1. For example, this is part of the reason why it is very difficult to reduce criminal penalties for some crimes even though many legislators may believe it would be good policy to do so.

Chapter Four

The Congressional Bubble

*"No man, however strong, can serve ten
years as schoolmaster, priest, or senator,
and remain fit for anything else."*

Henry Adams

*"I don't want any 'yes-men' around me.
I want everybody to tell me the truth
even if it costs them their jobs."*

Samuel Goldwyn

Remember how our fictional Rick Johnson's life changed when he got to Congress. Everyone he met knew his name and wanted to become friends with him. The attention that lobbyists gave his policy ideas thrilled him. His staff responded politely and positively to most suggestions he made. Finally, he was getting the respect he had long felt he deserved.

Johnson's story illustrates how members live in a bubble that they have collectively created. Life in that bubble differs from real life as other people experience it. Members get special treatment everywhere they go. After a time, this way of life begins to feel normal. But it disconnects them from their constituents. Their ambition and self-confidence, which are already larger than most people's, tend to grow inside this bubble just as plants grow inside a greenhouse. Over time, members can get so disconnected that they drift away from what their constituents actually want and substitute what the member wants. All the while, members seduce themselves into thinking that they know better what is good for the country. Placed in this kind of environment,

most human beings would react the same way. If no one ever tells us we are wrong, we begin to believe we are always right.

What are the elements of the bubble? First, serving as a member has become a full-time job. Congress now meets more or less year-round. The congressional schedule requires members to spend most of their time in Washington. Most members find it necessary to maintain a full-time residence in Washington to hold the job. Inevitably, despite all efforts to overcome it, this time away separates them from the daily lives of their constituents. Members have most of their conversations with other members and congressional staff rather than with the people who sent them. Their focus starts to shift from outside the Beltway to inside the Beltway.

When they get to Washington, they receive a government salary. That salary does not fluctuate with the business cycle. It comes steadily, irrespective of what is going on in the rest of the world. For purposes of their own finances, they need not worry about the vagaries of the economy. They know they will get paid, and they have no personal economic worries.

They also receive taxpayer funds to hire a staff. Within certain broad parameters, they are free to hire and fire whomever they choose. Those staffers know that the member can let them go at any time for any reason. For that reason, most staff find it hard to tell a member that he is wrong. The unusual self-confidence that members have only exacerbates the problem. Once a member disagrees with the advice of a staffer, the staffer's best course is to go along with the member's view if the staffer wants to keep his job.[1]

Much the same is true with the lobbyists whom the member meets with all day long. They all want something from the members. So lobbyists are loath to challenge the member's view of the world or tell him that he is wrong. Rather, they try to make their cases in a way that sounds like what they know the member already wants to hear.

Aside from never telling members no, staffers are always at the beck and call of members. Members rarely have to pick up their dry cleaning or make their own airline reservations. They get used to having other people do mundane tasks for them. This further removes them from normal life. For example, Senator Ben Nelson was quoted as saying that he did not know how to vote on a bill to cap automatic teller machine fees because he had never used one and did not know what the fees were.[2] Likewise, the first President Bush once let himself in for a round of criticism when he went to a grocery store and had to admit that he had never seen a bar code scanner. This sort of thing happens frequently on Capitol Hill.

Members lose track of the cost of things and the amount of effort it will take to produce a certain result. They begin to believe that resources are infinite. It is easy to see how that happens.

A person with a large ego, abundant energy, and a lot of self-confidence wins an election when everyone told him he could not. He begins to feel invincible. He comes to Washington and no one ever tells him he is wrong. He gets further and further away from his previous life and the people he knew there. Whatever thoughts pass through his head go unchallenged by those around him. Like any other human being in this situation, he begins to think that all his ideas are right, and that only reinforces the whole cycle. Feelings of invincibility and omnipotence then feed into a system of rules that tend to encourage partisan division. We turn to those now.

Endnotes

See all endnote links at <www.TCNABC.com>.

1. For more on the role of congressional staff, see *Persuading Congress*, Chapter 6.

2. "ATMs a Mystery to Senator," *Omaha World-Herald*, May 20, 2010.

Chapter Five

Procedures Designed to Divide

"A house divided against itself cannot stand."
Abraham Lincoln

"Congress is so strange. A man gets up to speak and says nothing. Nobody listens— and then everybody disagrees."
Boris Marshalov, Russian Writer

Rick Johnson quickly learned that minority party members have little opportunity to influence policy. He thought about it in business terms. He was not going to get any return on time invested in policy work. Though Johnson had some good friends in the majority party, he saw no benefit to working with them on their bills. That would help them keep their majority and consign Johnson to permanent minority status. Johnson was likely only going to enact his NFIP bill if his party won the majority, so that is where he invested most of his time. Most minority party members follow more or less the same course.

Why does this happen? Under current congressional procedures, members of the majority party decide almost all of the crucial questions before Congress. Most importantly, they almost completely control what their chambers will consider every day. William Marcy "Boss" Tweed, the legendary leader of the Tammany Hall political machine, reportedly said, "I don't care who does the electing, as long as I get to do the nominating." Much the same point applies to the selection of the congressional agenda. It does not really matter so much

that a member can vote if he has no control of what the questions will be.

In both chambers, members of the minority do have some powers they can use to slow down or stop the movement of legislation. In the Senate, the minority party can threaten to engage in extended debate.[1] The majority party must muster sixty votes to cut off the debate.[2] So long as the minority party has forty-one seats and its members vote together, it can stop any measure. The Massachusetts special election held in January 2010 illustrated this point. When Republican Senator Scott Brown unexpectedly won that election, he gave the minority Republicans a forty-first vote. That completely changed the dynamics in the Senate for the rest of 2010.

In theory, minority party senators also have the freedom to offer all kinds of amendments to bills on the Senate floor. The Senate rules do not require that amendments relate to the subject matter of the underlying bill.[3] Minority party members can use amendments to force their proposals on to the agenda. As a practical matter, however, the Senate majority leader has procedural tools at his disposal to effectively block the minority's efforts to offer amendments if he so chooses.[4]

Minority party representatives confront an even less satisfying situation in the House. The House majority determines what bills are considered both in committee and on the floor. When a bill comes up on the House floor, the majority party leadership exerts complete control over what amendments all other members can offer.

Only in committee can a minority party member in the House offer an amendment without the approval of at least some majority party members. Even then the amendment must relate to the same subject matter as the underlying bill. If you come up with a committee amendment that particularly troubles the majority, it may cut off your chance to offer it. It can simply skip committee consideration and take the bill directly to the floor. The minority does have some procedural tools by which it can slow things down or even force bills on to the agenda, but they can only succeed if at least some majority party members vote with them. It is a rare circumstance when the minority party can get that kind of support.[5]

The majority party also determines how the chambers will resolve differences between House and Senate bills. If a bill goes to a conference committee, the majority party members control all the action. For the most part, they need not even tell the minority party members what they are doing. The majority party may also choose to send amendments back and forth between the chambers rather than going to a conference committee. Whatever method the majority party chooses, the minority party has no say in the matter. It can only watch what happens and complain.[6]

Consider where this situation leaves a minority party member. Having done all that it took to win his seat, he comes to Congress and finds himself largely irrelevant to the policymaking process. In many cases, he may not know any more about what is going on behind the scenes on important legislation than the general public does. Yet he ran for the office because he wanted to get some of his policy ideas enacted into law.

The only good that comes of this situation is that the public does not hold him responsible for governing the country. Thus, he has a certain amount of freedom to investigate and advocate policy changes that a member of the majority party does not have. He can dabble in interesting new ideas without much cost because no one expects him to be able to enact them. Before the 1994 midterm election, the House Republicans used this freedom in their efforts to regain the majority. They would stay after hours and give speeches on C-SPAN about their ideas. Ultimately, they bundled some of them together in the party platform known as the Contract with America. By contrast, a majority party member might catch more flak for talking about the same ideas. In the majority, a member is expected to produce results, not give inconsequential speeches on C-SPAN.

Does the typical minority party member respond to this situation by thinking, "Well, I will just sit here, luxuriate in my freedom to be irrelevant, and have a good time going to parties"? Certainly not. Minor-

ity party members, like most human beings, respond to the obvious incentives in the situation. They look across the aisle, see how exciting life looks for their majority party colleagues, and decide that they want to get some of that good life for themselves.

That is how Rick Johnson saw it. He went to a couple of fundraisers and the next thing he knew, he was hooked. Like most minority party members, he quickly decided to focus most of his attention on trying to regain the majority in the next election. Minority party members do this in any number of ways, but most importantly for Congress's policy results, they refuse to cooperate with the majority party on legislative initiatives. Why help the majority party produce victories that will only help them maintain the majority and relegate you to minority party status for another two years? As legendary film producer Samuel Goldwyn said: "Include me out." Rather, members of the minority party do everything they can to trip up and embarrass the majority party.

Seen from the perspective of a minority party member, this lack of cooperation makes perfect sense. It is the fastest way to get to where you want to go. Seen from the perspective of a typical voter, it looks like two parties full of Nero-like politicians bickering endlessly while Rome burns around them.

Endnotes

See all endnote links at <www.TCNABC.com>.

1. To engage in extended debate in an effort to kill a bill is known as a "filibuster." See *Congressional Deskbook*, § 8.210 Consideration and Debate on the Senate Floor.

2. When sixty senators vote to cut off debate, the Senate is said to have "invoked cloture." See *Congressional Deskbook*, § 8.231 Steps to Invoke Cloture.

3. In parliamentary parlance, an amendment that relates to the same subject matter as the underlying bill is said to be "germane" to the bill. Generally speaking, in the House, amendments must be germane. In the Senate, amendments need not be germane except in very limited circumstances. (See <*www.CongressionalGlossary.com*>.)

4. This procedural tool is known as "filling the amendment tree." For more on Senate floor procedures, see *Congressional Deskbook*, §§ 8.160-8.250.

5. On most bills, the minority can offer an amendment by a motion to recommit, but it is usually defeated on a party line vote. For more on House floor procedures, see *Congressional Deskbook*, §§ 8.70-8.140.

6. For more on procedures for reconciling differences between the House and the Senate, see *Congressional Deskbook*, §§ 8.260-8.280.

Chapter Six

The Drive
for Reelection

*"I am persuaded that in the case of Congress,
the overwhelming temptation is to conclude that
it is more important for your constituents that
you be reelected than to deal honestly with them."*

Senator James L. Buckley (NY-R, 1971–1976)

*"The first instinct of power
is the retention of power."*

Justice Antonin Scalia,
Dissenting in *McConnell v. FEC* (2003)

et's face it. Despite many frustrations, members have pretty cushy jobs if they can hold on to them. Most members desperately want to do so. They view their seat as a career choice—as a full-time, long-term position—not a temporary one. Rick Johnson certainly saw it that way. He never even thought about not running for a second term. In his mind, he had left real estate behind and had embarked on a new career when he came to Congress. He wanted to hold on to his seat for as long as he could.

Much of the chaos in Congress arises from that view. To grasp that point, imagine what kinds of policies it would enact if none of its members cared about getting reelected. The place would certainly run differently. Members might even find a way to phase out programs like Rick Johnson's cherished NFIP rather than increasing its subsidies. As Ralph Waldo Emerson said, "There is no limit to what can be accomplished if it does not matter who gets the credit."

But in Congress, it matters very much who gets the credit and who gets the blame.[1] As discussed above, getting reelected requires mem-

bers to work constantly to increase their name recognition. Because members win reelection one vote at a time, they have a strong incentive to curry favor with even the smallest groups. This fosters an unhealthy tendency to focus on problems that affect only small groups at the expense of addressing the nation's larger problems. It also leads to many meaningless activities that pander to small groups.

Members engage in many activities designed to do this. For example, almost every major disease has a nonprofit organization dedicated to curing it. They do a lot of wonderful work. When such a group approaches a member, the member feels a strong temptation to support the group's request for public funding for research to cure that specific disease. The member gains nothing with this group by telling them about the bigger picture—that we have a finite number of dollars to spend on overall medical research. Finding the cure for any disease is a worthy cause. But somehow we must still allocate the overall pie rationally. The public as a whole would probably benefit from a comprehensive, rather than a disease-by-disease, approach.

An individual disease group does not want to hear that. They want to hear about what the member will do for their disease. This is a perfectly normal human feeling for someone who suffers from a disease or has a loved one who does. The member cannot risk being charged with being against research for the particular organization's disease. So he agrees to address the problem individually.[2] When Rick Johnson became a serial cosponsor, he signed on to every single disease bill. For him, it was the rational and productive thing to do. And besides, the money was not coming out of his pocket, so why not support every group's request and win the gratitude of its members?

This problem repeats itself in a wide variety of other areas. Everyone's actions make sense from an individual perspective, but collectively they do not make sense for the public at large. NFIP worked much the same way. People who already had homes in flood plains needed the program to continue. The rest of the public probably would have benefited more from spending the money elsewhere.

Even when members cannot do something meaningful for a group, they have many ways of taking meaningless actions to show their affinity with a group. For example, Rick Johnson showed support for his hometown employer by sponsoring a resolution declaring "National Frozen Food Week." Or they can burnish their credentials with a particular ethnic group by voting to name a post office after one of its prominent members. Such actions generally do not harm anyone. They are the political equivalent of putting a bumper sticker on your car. But they are not cost-free. It takes a certain amount of time and resources to pass even these minor types of bills. They may make the individual group feel good, but they have little meaning for the populace at large. Members pass them to boost their reelection efforts, and organized interests like them because they are tangible successes to show their members. As the frozen food lobbyist told Johnson, it gave him something tangible to show the CEO that his efforts were working.

To get a feel for this, consider these statistics. The 110th Congress met in 2007-08 and passed 460 public laws. Of those, 146 had no other purpose than to rename some public facility after a person. Another 18 were other forms of commemoration. Thus, over a third (36 percent) of all the laws that Congress passed honored some person or group, but did nothing else. Another 51 (11 percent) were mere extensions of current law with little or no significant change to the underlying policy. Together these two categories made up almost half of the laws that Congress passed during those two years.[3]

No doubt all of the people commemorated were worthy of the honor. And no doubt all of the laws needed extending. But the two categories make up a very high percentage of Congress's work product for a two-year session. It raises the question of whether we are getting our money's worth out of keeping Congress in Washington full time.

Endnotes

See all endnote links at <www.TCNABC.com>.

1. For more on members' desire for credit, see *Persuading Congress*, Chapter 18.
2. The 110th Congress, which sat in 2007-08, enacted eleven laws that related either to a specific disease or medical problem or a small cluster of them. National Breast and Cervical Cancer Early Detection Program Reauthorization Act of 2007,

Pub. L. No. 110-18, 121 Stat. 80 (2007); An Act to Amend Title 39, United States Code, to Extend the Authority of the United States Postal Service to Issue a Semipostal to Raise Funds for Breast Cancer Research, Pub. L. No. 110-150, 121 Stat. 1820 (2007); Newborn Screening Saves Lives Act of 2007, Pub. L. No. 110-204, 122 Stat. 705 (2008); Traumatic Brain Injury Act of 2008, Pub. L. No. 110-206, 122 Stat. 714 (2008); Caroline Pryce Walker Conquer Childhood Cancer Act of 2008, Pub. L. No. 110-285, 122 Stat. 2628 (2008); Tom Lantos and Henry J. Hyde United States Global Leadership Against HIV/AIDS, Tuberculosis, and Malaria Reauthorization Act of 2008, Pub. L. No. 110-293, 122 Stat. 2918 (2008); Breast Cancer and Environmental Research Act of 2008, Pub. L. No. 110-354, 122 Stat. 3984 (2008); Paul D. Wellstone Muscular Dystrophy Community Assistance, Research, and Education Amendments Act of 2008, Pub. L. No. 110-361, 122 Stat. 4010 (2008); ALS Registry Act, Pub. L. No. 110-373, 122 Stat. 4047 (2008); Prenatally and Postnatally Diagnosed Conditions Awareness Act, Pub. L. No. 110-374, 122 Stat. 4051 (2008); Comprehensive Tuberculosis Elimination Act, Pub. L. No. 110-392, 122 Stat. 4195 (2008). See Appendix A for an explanation of how these numbers were derived.

3. See Appendix A for an explanation of how these numbers were derived.

Chapter Seven

"Accomplishments"

"Horsemanship through the history of all nations has been considered one of the highest accomplishments. You can't pass a park without seeing a statue of some old codger on a horse."
Will Rogers

"Knowledge may give weight, but accomplishments give luster and many more people see than weigh."
Herodotus

The quest to get credit for accomplishments to fuel reelection bids goes well beyond meaningless actions. That is only the beginning. It also has more harmful forms.

Representatives face election every two years and senators every six. Unfortunately, the right environment to pass wise policy solutions comes around less frequently. In the interim, members must run their reelection campaigns anyway. As they do so, they face the inevitable voter questions about "what have you done for me lately?" They want to have something to point to rather than staring blankly back at the crowd.

The visualization of that deer in the headlights moment creates the desire for "accomplishments." Rick Johnson felt that he had to inoculate himself against that moment. No matter what else happened, he could always talk about his NFIP bill. That was something that would put money in the pockets of a lot of his voters. The idea proved a winner through thick and thin. The only problem was that it had not gone anywhere yet.

As legislators, members accomplish something by passing new laws. Like the man with a hammer who sees every problem as a nail, legislators tend to see every problem as something that requires a new law. They tend to define each new law as an "accomplishment" regardless of its actual effect.

In the same vein, they tend to see every effort to pass a law that does not succeed as a "failure." That is not always the case. Some problems solve themselves while bills are pending. That may happen because of market dynamics, court decisions, technological breakthroughs, or any number of other external factors. Often these factors may make a proposed law hopelessly outdated before it even passes, or shortly thereafter.

When members pass a law that does not work, they tend to tinker with it further rather than repeal it. That is exactly what Johnson's bill would have done to NFIP. Only rarely does anyone in Congress see getting rid of an obsolete law or program as an accomplishment. Sheila Wilkinson would have been such a rare bird. Most members implicitly assume that all laws and government programs should continue in perpetuity. Or at a minimum, they feel that getting rid of those things carries too much political cost. Wilkinson would not have assumed that and she would have made her thoughts explicit—but she did not run.

In real life, however, the best legislative response to many problems is to do nothing. As noted, many problems work themselves out in time. Government intervention often tends to prolong the problem rather than relieve it. Certainly, NFIP encouraged the building of homes in flood plains only to be destroyed again a few years later. Often removing or phasing out an existing government intervention like NFIP might help more than passing a new law that adds another government intervention.

This is not to say that all new laws or government interventions in the economy are harmful or unnecessary or that markets solve all problems. Quite the contrary, many laws are needed and they work well. Markets sometimes fail. But because of the drive for reelection, when Congress looks at a problem, it has a strong bias toward passing a new law. That often takes the form of a government intervention in the economy. The new law gives the members involved an "accomplishment" to tout back home—doing nothing does not. The actual substance of the law and its effect become secondary. Nothing must stand in the way of the "accomplishment."

This problem grows worse when the legislation at issue forms a central part of the agenda of the party in power. The fear of failing to pass the law and leaving egg all over the party's face can overwhelm all considerations of wise policy. Party leaders agree to whatever political deals must be made to get the necessary votes irrespective of the underlying policy. The legislation can morph into a monstrosity that looks nothing like its original version.

This mentality drove the Democrats' passage of the health care reform legislation in 2009-10 as well as the Republicans' passage of a transportation appropriations bill in 2005 that included the infamous "Bridge to Nowhere."[1] The near manic desire to accomplish something left public concerns about the policy in the dust. Legislators seeking reelection hoped that voters would see Herodotus's luster around them without weighing the policy involved. In both these cases, however, the legislation contributed to an electoral disaster. Voters weighed the policy and found it wanting.

Endnotes

See all endnote links at <www.TCNABC.com>.

1. Patient Protection and Affordable Care Act, Pub. L. No. 111-148, 124 Stat. 119 (2010); Transportation, Treasury, Housing and Urban Development, The Judiciary, The District of Columbia, and Independent Agencies Appropriations Act, 2006, Pub. L. No. 109-115, 119 Stat. 2396 (2005).

Chapter Eight

Crisis: An Opportunity to Waste

"The crisis of today is the joke of tomorrow."

H.G. Wells

"Any idiot can face a crisis, it is this day-to-day living that wears you out."

Anton Chekhov

The drive for reelection can also lead to unnecessary or ill-considered legislation in a variety of situations that members perceive as crises.[1] This problem has several aspects.

The first is whether a crisis actually exists. As one veteran Capitol Hill staffer told me, "There are no true emergencies on Capitol Hill—just perceived emergencies." Usually, members perceive that a crisis exists because the press is reporting about a problem. Persistent press focus on a story often stampedes members into thinking they need to do something about it. In that situation, it does not take long for members to realize that they can get press coverage by "responding" to the perceived crisis. But a "response" needs to have some useful substance. Not yet knowing much about the facts, members often tout off-the-cuff policy ideas as their "response" to a crisis. They sound good for a moment and give the appearance that the member is doing something. But perceived crises evolve over time and often turn out differently than they first appear.

Remember the controversy about Toyota's gas pedals that roiled Congress in 2010? Toyota did have real problems with some vehicles, but the National Highway Traffic Safety Administration later found that

driver error caused many of the "stuck" accelerators.[2] By the time this information became public, the House Energy and Commerce Committee had already acted on its response to the situation, a comprehensive federal law—the "Motor Vehicle Safety Act of 2010."[3]

Much the same is true of the British Petroleum oil spill in the spring and summer of 2010. The underwater views of oil leaking into the Gulf of Mexico dominated television screens for several months and spurred numerous congressional hearings. The spill undoubtedly ranked as an environmental disaster of the first order. But early predictions of enormous long-term damage may have overstated the problem. It turns out that, among other things, microbes are eating some of the spilled oil.[4] Again, by the time this information became public, the House Energy and Commerce Committee had already acted on its response, another new federal law—the "Blowout Prevention Act of 2010."[5] It is too early to say, but the moratorium on drilling that the administration instituted to respond to the leak may ultimately cause more long-term economic damage than the spill itself.[6]

Both of these situations involved serious issues that warranted congressional attention. The point here is that the situations changed as more facts came in. Because of the desire to get favorable press attention, members rushed to the cameras with all kinds of proposals to "respond" before they had a clear idea of what caused the problem. As the facts became clearer, these immediate crises melted into persistent, long-term problems. In such situations, a thoughtful solution developed over time will almost always serve the country better than a hastily drafted crisis "response."

A closely related aspect of this problem is members' fear of doing nothing. When press reports convince the public that a crisis is afoot, legislators want to do something. Usually, that something is to pass a new law. But it is often quite unclear that the proposed new law would have prevented the crisis had it previously been in place. Likewise, it is often unclear that going forward, the proposed new law will improve the situation. Even if the best response is to do nothing, the fear of inaction drives members to do something regardless of its efficacy.

Crises also create opportunities to enact policy options that partisans have long desired, but have not passed. As former White House Chief of Staff Rahm Emanuel, once a member himself, put it shortly after the 2008 election: "You never want a serious crisis to go to waste. . . . Things that we had postponed for too long, that were long-term, are now immediate and must be dealt with. And this crisis provides the opportunity for us . . . to do things that you could not do before."[7]

His statement embodies another aspect of the congressional approach to crisis by both major parties. The key part of the statement is things that you could not do before. Other ideas may have had a greater claim on limited resources, or perhaps some significant part of the public opposed doing the idea. But the idea failed for a reason. In the crisis mentality that frequently engulfs Congress, those reasons often get pushed aside.

Rick Johnson prepared for just such a moment. He knew that if major floods hit anywhere in the country and the press paid a lot of attention to them, then Congress would probably scramble to act on NFIP reform. He had told his staff to be ready for such a moment. By talking about his bill frequently, he had positioned himself well to own the issue should a crisis arise. Until his party won the majority back, this kind of situation was probably the only way that he would get his bill enacted. If the moment arose, Johnson was ready to pounce.

Likewise, as a response to the financial crisis of late 2008, Congress passed a fiscal stimulus bill in early 2009.[8] It contained numerous spending items that would never have passed if they had been considered individually on their own merits. One section provided $8 billion to build intercity high-speed rail projects.[9] Had this project gone through the normal appropriations process, it would never have attracted that amount of money. But the economic problems of that moment created an environment that allowed almost any amount of spending to pass for almost any purpose.

Lawyers often say that hard cases make bad law. No matter how hard the case is, a court has to resolve it somehow. The result is often

not pretty. The same idea applies to Congress in a crisis. In members' minds, they must do something, irrespective of whether there is anything good to do.

Endnotes

See all endnote links at <www.TCNABC.com>.

1. For more on the crisis mentality in Congress, see *Persuading Congress*, Chapter 40.

2. *See* "Early Tests Pin Toyota Accidents on Drivers," by Mike Ramsey and Kate Linebaugh, *The Wall Street Journal*, July 13, 2010.

3. See H.R. 5381, 111th Cong. (2010), ordered reported on May 26, 2010. H. Rep. No. 111-536 (2010).

4. See "No Dead Zones Observed or Expected as Part of BP Deepwater Horizon Oil Spill," NOAA press release, September 7, 2010.

5. See H.R. 5626, 111th Cong. (2010), ordered reported on July 15, 2010. H. Rep. No. 111-581, Part 1 (2010).

6. On October 12, 2010, the administration lifted the moratorium, but the oil industry expressed concern that it might be continued as a practical matter because of permitting delays. See "API Pleased with Moratorium Lift, But Concerned about De Facto Ban," American Petroleum Institute press release, October 12, 2010.

More broadly, both parties and all congressional committees fall victim to the urge to legislate before all the facts are in about a perceived crisis. The House Energy and Commerce Committee just happens to have provided two good recent examples. With regard to the long-term damage of the drilling moratorium, see Chapter 18 below.

7. See video of Mr. Emanuel's comment on YouTube, "Rahm Emanuel on the Opportunities of Crisis."

8. American Recovery and Reinvestment Act, Pub. L. No. 111-5, 123 Stat. 115 (2009).

9. See 123 Stat. at 208. At the time, this provision caused controversy because critics charged that despite the facial neutrality of the language, Senate Majority Leader Harry Reid of Nevada inserted the provision to fund a Las Vegas to Los Angeles high-speed train. Whatever the merits of that charge, it is beside the point here.

Chapter Nine

Third Rails

*"Social Security is a government program
with a constituency made up of the old, the
near old, and those who hope or fear to grow old.
After 215 years of trying, we have finally discovered
a special interest that includes 100 percent of the
population. Now we can vote ourselves rich."*

P. J. O'Rourke

*"The question isn't at what age I want to retire,
it's at what income."*

George Foreman

irk O'Donnell, an aide to Speaker Tip O'Neill, first referred to
Social Security as the third rail of American politics in the early
1980s. He meant that any member touching it would die politically. Social Security, Medicare, Medicaid, and a variety of other federal government entitlement programs all pulse with political current.
Millions of citizens depend on them. Their anger would electrocute the
career of any politician who tried to take them away.

Despite wishes to the contrary, we cannot indefinitely sustain
many of these programs in their current forms. The Social Security and
Medicare Board of Trustees repeatedly reports that these programs will
become insolvent in coming years.[1] Yet Congress does nothing to reform them. Finding solutions that would get them back on track requires little technical expertise. That is relatively easy to do. If Congress were willing to raise the retirement age a few years, it could easily
make Social Security solvent again.

But purely political considerations bar such solutions from polite conversation. Members seeking reelection want to avoid these third rails at all costs. They fear that political opponents will attack them for candidly discussing what can be done. The issues involved are hard to explain, but easy to demagogue.

For example, some Republicans have suggested that Congress could strengthen Social Security's solvency by using a different formula to calculate cost-of-living adjustments.[2] Try explaining the difference between "progressive price indexing" and "wage indexing" to a group of senior citizens when an opponent is telling them that it means a cut to their hard-earned benefits. During consideration of the health care reform law, some Democrats proposed that Medicare should pay for end-of-life planning consultations with doctors. Try explaining that to senior citizens when your opponents are saying that the consultations are "death panels" designed to convince you to euthanize yourself.[3]

Because members want to win reelection, they cannot resist the temptation to engage in this kind of demagoguery. It pays easy political dividends. One need only remember the 1989 video of former Ways and Means Chairman Dan Rostenkowski being chased to his car by senior citizens angry over another Medicare reform to see why this is so.[4] By contrast, trying to address these kinds of issues risks political suicide and yields little reward.

In an effort to address the entitlement programs and other deficit issues, President Obama signed an executive order on February 18, 2010, that established a bipartisan commission to make recommendations on entitlement reform.[5] The order required the Commission to vote on its recommendations by December 1, 2010. But months before that date, Democratic senators began saying publicly that they would not accept a variety of options that the commission might suggest. Senator Bernie Sanders of Vermont, along with 11 cosponsors, introduced a non-binding resolution rejecting any privatization of Social Security or any increase in the retirement age.[6] In the same vein, when Democrats tried to establish the commission by statute, many Republicans rejected the suggestion out of hand, claiming that it would only provide cover for tax increases. The substantive merits of those positions go beyond the purview of this book. But the unwillingness of senators of both parties to let a commission even try to devise politically viable solutions demonstrates the difficulty of dealing with these issues.

Most of the members involved have now safely won reelection, but the fiscal time bomb keeps ticking. Congress has shown no willingness to defuse it; however, reform must come sooner or later. If Congress changes its ways, it can shape that reform in advance. If it does not, it will have to pick up the pieces after the fiscal bomb explodes.

Endnotes

See all endnote links at <www.TCNABC.com>.

1. The Reports about Social Security and Medicare are available from the Board of Trustees at: *<www.ssa.gov/OACT/TR/>*.

2. See Rep. Paul Ryan's "A Roadmap for America's Future."

3. See "Palin vs. Obama: Death Panels," FactCheck.org, August 14, 2009.

4. See the video clip, " 'Buried In The Archives,' The Original Town-Hall Battle," CBS News, August 10, 2009, on YouTube.

5. See Executive Order 13531, National Commission on Fiscal Responsibility and Reform, 75 FR 7927, February 18, 2010.

6. S. Res. 664, 111th Cong. (2010). See related press release, "Congress Steps Up to Protect Social Security," from Sen. Bernie Sanders, September 30, 2010.

Part II

How to Fix Congress

A. Solutions for Both Chambers
Chapters 10–16

B. Solutions Specific to the Senate
Chapters 17–18

C. Solutions Specific to the House
Chapters 19–20

Chapter Ten

Temporary Duty

*"One thing our founding fathers could not foresee . . .
was a nation governed by professional politicians who
have a vested interest in getting reelected. They probably
envisioned a fellow serving a couple of hitches and
then looking forward to getting back to the farm."*

Ronald Reagan

*"In retrospect, I wish I had known more about the hazards and
difficulties of such a business, especially during a recession. . . .
I also wish that during the years I was in public office I had had
this firsthand experience about the difficulties business people
face every day. That knowledge would have made me a better U.S.
senator and a more understanding presidential contender. . . .
But my business associates and I also lived with federal, state
and local rules that were all passed with the objective of helping
employees, protecting the environment, raising tax dollars for
schools, protecting our customers from fire hazards. While I have
never doubted the worthiness of any of those goals, the concept
that most often eludes legislators is: 'Can we make consumers
pay the higher prices for the increased operating costs that
accompany public regulation and government reporting
requirements with reams of red tape?' It is a simple
concern that nonetheless legislators often ignore."*

George McGovern, on running an inn

U nder current rules, serving in Congress is a full-time job. The responsibilities require far more than forty hours of work a week and the salary reflects that. New members must relinquish their previous jobs because of the sheer demands of holding office and ethics rules that generally prevent them from earning income other than their congressional salaries.[1]

A member's life is not easy—it is hard work. But compared to working in the private sector, it is easier in some ways. No market force can eliminate the member's guaranteed paycheck. He never has to borrow money to make payroll or pay for higher employee benefit costs. A member knows that his employees will always get paid and have great benefits regardless of what he does.

By contrast, business people confront a daily maelstrom of competitive forces. Sometimes they are up; sometimes they are down. Forces beyond their control buffet them constantly. They must always worry that the competition is gaining on them or that some unforeseen event could destroy their livelihood. For business people, actions have consequences.

Members experience daily life differently. When they meet with someone, they almost always have the upper hand. When people meet with a member, they usually need something from the member—not vice versa. Remember that Rick Johnson did not want to go back to selling real estate precisely because the people on the other side of the table did not need him there. Over time, that warps their perspective on how the world works.

That is bad enough, but the full-time nature of Congress has several other distorting effects. As discussed in Chapters 1 and 2, many capable people do not run for Congress because the time commitment precludes it. They simply cannot give up their current responsibilities. Absent that bar, more candidates would run and that would make congressional elections more competitive.

Congress currently meets year-round with occasional short breaks. To be present for all votes, members must necessarily spend much of their time in Washington. Thus, they live much of their life in the bubble. As members spend more time in Washington, they lose perspective on the situation in their districts. Members do not make this change intentionally—it just inevitably results from not living a normal life located in their district.

When members are in Washington, they feel the need to do Washington things—hold hearings, conduct oversight, introduce bills—to justify their time there and to generate favorable press coverage. Having all this time to fill creates a competitive race to the bottom. Members identify more and more "problems" that require legislative solutions, so they can rack up more and more "accomplishments." This overactive policymaking does not guarantee better quality. At any given time, a relatively small number of wise and necessary policy ideas are floating around Congress. As members stay in Washington longer and feel the need to generate activity, the quality of most of their ideas tends to decline, but their level of activity does not.

As Congress stays in session longer, its own costs of doing business increase while it produces diminishing returns. The process for passing many bills gets drawn out because nothing forces a conclusion. Knowing that more time is available, members see no reason to come to agreement. Members hold up bills for months without negotiating seriously. The bills grow ever more complex because the members have the time to make them so. Toward the end of a session, members suddenly see the need to wrap things up and they start a headlong rush to close their deals. The result often approximates a ten-car pileup.

Now suppose that members looked at their government service differently—the way the average citizen does. To take two common examples, average citizens serve the government in the military and on juries. In those cases, the citizen typically sees that service as a duty—perhaps even a burden—but not an opportunity to get into a more enjoyable line of work for life. They tend to look at it with the attitude that "it's a dirty job, but someone has to do it." With that attitude, they complete the job and get on with their lives.

How could we make Congress more like military service or jury duty? First, Congress should shorten its sessions. In the days before air conditioning, the country prospered with Congress meeting just a few months a year. Shorter sessions would force narrower agendas, quicker decisions, and simpler laws.

Second, we need to reduce congressional pay and let members work full-time jobs elsewhere to make their living. Nothing would keep

them more grounded. The George McGovern quote above illustrates the point nicely. Most state legislatures work this way, and they rarely get as far afield from what the public wants as Congress does.

This is not an argument that members are overpaid.[2] Being a member is hard work, and we want good people to serve there. To achieve that, we have to pay members well. Rather, the argument is that a full-time system has grown up over the years, and it encourages bad results. We will get better results if serving in Congress becomes part-time, rather than full-time, work. In a part-time system, we must pay good part-time wages. But those wages must ensure that members need their other jobs.

Imagine how much more quickly Congress would work if members had to get back home to their jobs. Imagine how much better informed their decisions would become if they worked in the same kinds of jobs that other Americans do. They might vote in the interests of their own business or employer, but at least that vote would rest on current real world experience.

Aside from those positive effects, such a system would also make it possible for many more people to run competitive races. If incumbents had to hold down full-time jobs, the challengers would start on a much more level playing field. With the demands of holding down another job, members would likely serve fewer terms. All of this should generate a wider pool of candidates, more turnover, and more intellectual ferment. We should get a more consistent level of talent in the Congress. That should in turn lead to better legislative results.

Think back to our fictional Rick Johnson's race. He won his seat in part because his strongest potential opponent, Sheila Wilkinson, decided not to run. She did not want to leave her children and her life full-time to serve in Congress. She might have decided to run in a part-time system. Her business partner had made it work in the state legislature. Had she run, she might have gone to Washington instead of Johnson. She might have contributed some quality ideas for a few terms and then let someone else have a shot. Not being a lifer, she might have voted for wiser policies than Johnson, who wanted the job for life.

Could members actually manage to hold down full-time jobs while serving in a part-time Congress? It would not be easy. As noted in Chapter 2, even today a person cannot realistically run for Congress unless they can afford to give up their job for a one- to two-year period. So they come to Congress with some ability to manage this, but today the need to do it is temporary. Once they are elected, they are set with a new job.

State legislatures that use this system usually have a set date by which they must adjourn. Thus, their members only have to manage the dual burden for part of the year.

But Congress differs in at least two significant ways that would make this harder for members. For most parts of the country, Washington is a lot further away from home than the state capital. And most members of Congress represent far more people than a member of a state legislature.

The travel would certainly take a physical toll on a member who also had to work a full-time job. But members endure that toll now, and under a part-time system, there would be fewer trips. The bigger issue for an employee or a business owner is how much time they have to spend away from their work. Leaders can manage that by only requiring members to be in Washington when they have important work to do. Certainly this kind of system would increase the pressure on leaders to do that.

As far as the much larger constituencies, staff handles most of the constituent service work now. Using a part-time system need not change that.[3] In addition, with a member spending more time in the district, he would have more time to focus on constituent service work.

Is it realistic to think that members would actually allow these changes to happen? Only if the public demands it. How could it happen? Shorter sessions can happen relatively easily. We only need strong leaders in both chambers to determine that this is the best course. If they do so, they can make it happen.

How we could change to lower, part-time salaries for members is much harder to imagine. Members would have to pass a law reducing

their own salaries. It is unlikely that this would happen in the short term. A package of congressional reforms of this magnitude could only take effect some years down the road to attract the votes of current members, many of whom want to protect their careers. A gradual decrease in salary could be implemented in exchange for a gradual increase in the amount of outside income that members can legally earn.

Another potential feature of this system might be to tie congressional pay to the shorter sessions. It could work in the following manner. By statute, Congress could set a target adjournment date for each year—say May 31. For every day before that date that Congress adjourns with all regular appropriations bills enacted into law, members get a daily bonus in their paychecks. For each day the session extends beyond that day, they get a deduction from their pay.

These ideas would transform members' current incentives and change the way they think about their jobs—but they only begin the conversation. Let's now turn to how members finance their campaigns.

Endnotes

See all endnote links at <www.TCNABC.com>.

1. See Rule XXV, Rules of the United States House of Representatives; Rule XXXVI, Rules of the United States Senate.

2. In 2010, members earned an annual salary of $174,000 and received the full panoply of federal government employment benefits. In the First Congress in 1789, they made $6 per day. As late as 1990, they made less than $100,000 per year. See <*www.CongressPay.com*>.

But the absolute numbers are somewhat misleading. Consider this from "Seven Ways to Compute the Relative Value of a U.S. Dollar Amount, 1774 to Present," MeasuringWorth.com: "George Washington was paid a salary of $25,000 a year from 1789 to 1797 as the first president of the United States. The current salary of the president has recently been doubled to $400,000, to go with a $50,000 expense account, a generous pension and several other benefits. Has the remuneration improved? Making a comparison using the CPI for 1790 shows that $25,000 corresponds to over $585,000 today, so the recent raise means current presidents have an equal command over consumer goods as the Father of the Country."

3. In Chapter 12 below, this book advocates cutting back on the number of congressional policy staff. If a part-time system were implemented, members would need to keep an adequate number of staff to perform constituent services such as academy appointments, Capitol flags, and help with federal agencies.

Chapter Eleven

All Cards on the Table

"Sunshine is the best disinfectant."

Louis Brandeis

"Bad laws are the worst sort of tyranny."

Edmund Burke

Our current campaign finance laws grew out of the Watergate scandal in the 1970s. Their supporters enacted them with the best of intentions. They believed that campaign contributions necessarily corrupted politicians. From their perspective, a law limiting contributions would limit political corruption. If only it were that simple. Unfortunately, the law now limits those contributions in a complex way that creates a host of unintended consequences.

In current practice, the campaign finance laws protect incumbents, create pointless traps for the unwary, and require candidates to spend inordinate amounts of time raising money. They also prevent those who are not skilled in large-scale fundraising from ever winning an election. On top of those unintended consequences, they limit everyone's First Amendment rights.

Let's look at each aspect of this problem in turn. Are campaign contributions necessarily corrupting? Interestingly, the most celebrated recent cases of congressional corruption involved members who took straight cash bribes—not campaign contributions. For example, former Representative Duke Cunningham of California actually maintained a "bribe menu" that showed what official actions he would take in exchange for different amounts of cash.[1] Former Representative William Jefferson allegedly kept $90,000 of bribe cash in his freezer.[2] Both of these members were ultimately convicted of corruption.

But it is much harder to tell if campaign contributions are corrupting. Almost every member takes contributions from organized interests. Every member then has to vote on legislation that affects those same interests. But which comes first? Does the politician vote a certain way because of a contribution or does the contribution come because the organized interest knows he would have voted that way regardless? Unfortunately, we cannot know the answer to that question. It probably differs from situation to situation. The interests and the politicians themselves may not even know the answer. Each side may have its own unspoken interpretation of what is happening.

Because some will always believe it, let's assume for the sake of argument that campaign contributions at least sometimes corrupt politicians. It is not clear that our current system is the best way of dealing with that problem. A less complicated and less costly method of ferreting out corruption would be to let voters judge. Using their collective knowledge of each individual situation would at a minimum cost far less than the current system.

Put aside the corruption aspect for a moment and consider the practical effects of the relatively low contribution limits that current law sets. As discussed in Chapters 1 and 2, the limits necessarily mean that candidates, whether they are incumbents or challengers, must spend large amounts of their time raising money if they want to compete on a level playing field.

For incumbents, that is time that they cannot spend making wise policy. For challengers, that is a strong disincentive to running at all. If they do take the plunge, it is time that they cannot spend developing good policy ideas. Moreover, if one believes that all contributions are corrupting, then it can be argued that this system merely increases the number of people to whom politicians are beholden. The idea was to lessen that number.

We have noted above that the burden of raising this money is so great that it works to protect incumbents in a variety of ways. Apart from the burden, to win an election, a candidate simply must have the skills necessary to raise all this money in small increments. Many people do not have those skills. For that reason, they are not going to become members of Congress. Thus, these laws eliminate a large number of people from contention even though some of them might be wise policymakers.

Then there is the complexity of the law. Any law ought to be simple enough that well-intentioned, ordinary people can comply with it. That cannot be said of current campaign finance law. It sets up numerous pointless traps for the unwary. For example, any invitation to a political fund-raiser must include certain disclaimers or it does not comply with the law.[3] It is hard to see how this serves any useful purpose.

On a more theoretical level, even assuming contribution limits are desirable, why can a political action committee give more to a campaign than an individual? Why should a group of people who make up a corporation or a union have to hide behind the fiction of a political action committee to give money collectively? Is there any real theoretical justification for any of this or is it simply arbitrary regulation?

Finally, if you care enough about a particular candidate's election to give him $50,000 or $100,000 of your own money, Congress should not limit your ability to communicate about a campaign through your chosen candidate. You have a First Amendment right to speak and associate with others for political purposes.

We can vastly simplify these laws while also ridding ourselves of many of their ill effects. Campaigns cost money and that is not going to change. We are never going to eliminate money from politics. There is too much at stake.

Allow unlimited contributions from all domestic sources and require candidates to disclose them immediately on the Internet. Get rid of PACs, independent expenditure groups, joint committees, and all the other arcane, expensive, and inexplicable apparatus of current law. They make up a system that only a bureaucrat could love. More importantly, they are not fooling anyone or keeping money out of politics.

In the age of the Internet, voters can easily find members' votes on legislation and judge for themselves whether they are corrupt. We

can also prohibit cash contributions and foreign contributions to prevent corruption. Virginia has such a system for its state elections, and it is perceived to be one of the least corrupt state political systems.[4]

What are the benefits? Such a system would free up a great deal of time for incumbents and challengers, encourage more candidates to run, and lower compliance costs. It would also allow people who are not skilled at fund-raising to run if they could find a few large contributors. Likewise, a small, but brave group of large contributors could combine their resources to bankroll a challenge to an entrenched incumbent—something that is not possible today. Congress can only benefit from less time spent on fund-raising and more competition in elections. We could have a much more robust debate if these pointless and unsuccessful laws were reduced to something more rational.

Is it realistic to think that members will vote to eliminate the current system? Probably not. It has too many incumbent protection benefits. However, as campaign costs continue to rise, the time issue grows worse. Eventually, the sheer amount of time that incumbents must spend raising money may at least force Congress to raise the contribution limits. Any step in that direction would improve the current nightmare.

Endnotes

See all endnote links at <www.TCNABC.com>.

1. The facts, including the "bribe menu," are described in the Justice Department's Sentencing Memo in "United States v. Randall Harold ('Duke') Cunningham, Government's Sentencing Memorandum, February 17, 2006" (Criminal Case No. 05cr2137-LAB in U.S. District Court, Southern District of California).

2. See "Congressman William Jefferson Indicted On Bribery, Racketeering, Money Laundering, Obstruction of Justice, and Related Charges," Dept. of Justice Press Release, June 4, 2007.

3. For more on the required disclaimers, see "Federal Election Campaign Guide: Congressional Candidates and Committees," Chapter 10, Conducting the Campaign (April 2008). Likewise, whether certain advertising is unregulated issue advocacy or regulated express advocacy turns on the use of certain "magic words" like "vote for," "elect." See *Buckley v. Valeo*, 424 U.S. 1, 44 n. 52 (1976).

4. *See generally* web site of the Virginia State Board of Elections, and "Virginia Campaign Finance Disclosure (CFDA)." According to NCSL, nine other states have similar laws. See "State Limits on Contributions to Candidates, Updated January 20, 2010."

Chapter Twelve

Back to Reality

> *"In free governments, the rulers are the servants and the people their superiors. For the former to return among the latter does not degrade, but rather promotes them."*
>
> Benjamin Franklin

> *"If you would have a faithful servant, and one that you like, serve yourself."*
>
> Benjamin Franklin

In Chapters 1, 2, and 4, we catalogued all of the taxpayer-funded resources that a member has and noted that these resources give incumbents a big advantage when they seek reelection. They make it harder for challengers and they therefore make elections less competitive. But the extraordinary growth of these resources, especially the number of staff, negatively affects the internal workings of Congress as well.[1]

Members need some of these resources to provide good representation to their constituents. But Congress managed its work for many years with little staff and few of the other resources. Only in the last 50 years or so has the number of staff exploded. Looking back on that period, it is not at all clear that the quality of work in Congress has increased. One could argue that the opposite is true. Do we really need three large office buildings full of staff to service a hundred senators? Or four large office buildings to service 435 representatives? If so, what are we paying the members to do?

The staff creates much of the bubble around members. Members tend to be unusually self-confident to begin with, and the staff echo

chamber around them only strengthens their original views. In that environment, members tend to question their own views less and less often.

The staff treatment goes well beyond policy matters. Everyone who works around Congress yields to members. Pleasant greetings are exchanged, doors are opened, dry cleaning is picked up, and the list goes on. In this kind of environment, any human being would naturally lose some perspective on things.

Staffers also fend off all manner of unpleasantness from constituents. This insulates members from what the public is thinking. When a member hears only the pleasant things that constituents have to say, they think everyone is happy.

Technology only worsens this effect. Members can now conduct town halls by simultaneous telephone calls to thousands of constituents. This technology allows members to reach more people, but it can also create a buffer effect. The member never really has to look his constituents in the eye. Likewise, telephone messages that members can record and send out to thousands of people give the illusion of intimacy while actually inhibiting it.

If they are so inclined, members can travel the world on the taxpayers' dime. One can make an argument that travel enlightens members and that they do a better job as a result. Seeing things first-hand can certainly give someone a new perspective on an issue. This is particularly true for war zones. However, my guess is that most hard-pressed taxpayers would gladly give up the supposed benefits of most congressional foreign travel in exchange for having the money spent on that travel returned to them. Moreover, time not spent on travel is time that can be spent on wise policymaking.

Will members vote to pop the bubble that surrounds them? It would require a majority of members to vote to make any change. Members are not going to vote to substantially reduce their resources under the current system. But a different system might provide a sufficient incentive for them to agree to some reduction while also increasing their accountability.

Here is how it could work. First, reduce the overall budget of each chamber by the largest percentage that can command the necessary votes. Then divide up the smaller budget among members according to the number of constituents they represent, as is done now. Eliminate all committee budgets and all budgets for other legislative offices. Put all spending decisions in the hands of the individual member.

Then allow members greater freedom to spend that money. If they want to hire more staff, let them do it. If they want to spend their money on staff to work on a committee's business, let them do that. If they want to hire a professional legislative drafter or fund an office full of them, they can do so. If they would rather spend their allotment on travel, they can do that. If they want to spend it all on franked mail, fine.

But let them know that there is only one allotment per Congress and make them account for it. If they overspend their allotment, make them repay it out of their pockets. If necessary, garnish their wages. If they underspend, let them keep a percentage of the money saved as a performance bonus.

Such a system would change the way that Congress works. No longer would the big machine keep spending money the same old way over and over. Rather, members would have greater freedom—which gives them a reason to change—but they would have to divide money among competing priorities every Congress. This market-based allocation would force difficult choices and cut waste.

Endnotes

See all endnote links at <www.TCNABC.com>.

1. The author spent more than a decade of his life as a congressional staffer, and the argument here and in the next chapter, Chapter 13, is not a criticism of congressional staffers. The vast majority are dedicated public servants who toil away in obscurity for less money than they could make in the private sector. Rather, the concern is that their sheer numbers insulate members from reality and enable them to delve into more subjects than they can reasonably handle. See Committee on House Administration, Member's Handbook, Section 3: Staff: <*http://cha.house.gov/members_handbook.aspx*>; and "Legislative Branch Staffing 1954-2007," CRS Report for Congress R40056, October 15, 2008.

Chapter Thirteen

Focus, Focus, Focus

"This country has come to feel the same when Congress is in session as when the baby gets hold of a hammer."
Will Rogers

"Often he who does too much does too little."
Italian Proverb

When they are in Washington, members work frenetically. All day long they must run from one event or meeting to the next. This scattershot style of work partially explains Congress's poor record. With members having little time to think through policy, the results are often not what the public desires.

When Congress is in session, members ought to spend most of their time focusing on making wise policy rather than scurrying frantically from event to event. Some of the reforms discussed above would help. If the leaders shortened the sessions as advocated in Chapter 10, members would have plenty of time to think about reelection after the session adjourned.

If the sessions were shorter, the leaders of each chamber could focus members' attention further by publicly announcing a limited number of topics that Congress would address during that session. Then they could simply refuse to bring up bills that do not address those topics. In the Senate, recalcitrant members might try to bring up other topics through unrelated amendments. The majority leader would have to enforce his limit on the topics through complicated procedural tactics, but he could do it without any rules change.

In the House, the task would be easier. Its rules are already writ-

ten so that determined majority party leaders could easily enforce a limit on topics. Indeed, such a tactic might be a welcome relief for some members.

As the House operates now, the leaders often bring up bills simply because members are in Washington. Often they are waiting for the Senate to act on some bill. The House leaders feel pressure to put something on the floor to justify the members' presence. If, however, we went to a part-time Congress as suggested in Chapter 10, the pressure would be in the other direction. Members would want to be home attending to their other jobs rather than in Washington attending to meaningless legislation.

In Chapter 11, we looked at how the current campaign finance rules require members to spend an inordinate amount of their time raising campaign money. If Congress enacted the reforms advocated there, that time would be substantially reduced. We could further reduce that time by prohibiting members from raising campaign contributions while Congress is in session. A number of state legislatures operate under this system without any major problems.[1] At least one federal court of appeals has upheld such a statute against constitutional challenge.[2]

This need not become an unfair advantage to incumbents or an impediment to challengers. Congress could use it as a further incentive for shorter sessions. Prohibit all candidates from raising money during a shortened session. However, if Congress does not end its session by a target adjournment date, then let those who are not incumbents start raising money. But continue the prohibition on incumbents until Congress does adjourn.

Apart from giving members more time to think about wise policy, this system would have other good effects. It would reduce the actual influence of organized interests as well as improving appearances. It would shorten congressional campaigns and perhaps thereby entice more challengers to run.

Would members vote for this kind of law? It is hard to predict. If a courageous leader pushed it to a vote, members might find it hard to vote against. Thoughtful members might also conclude that on balance they benefit from it because a shortened fund-raising period might give them an advantage over challengers. Certainly a number of state legislators have voted for it. But good old-fashioned fear of change might also work to defeat it. In this case, we will not know until someone tries it.

In Chapter 12, we looked at the vast expansion of staff and how it insulates members. But it scatters their attention as well. The availability of so many staffers allows members to delve into every conceivable subject. Because members can, they do. More and more problems are identified; more and more hearings are held, and more and more bills are written. Members try to do everything, and they end up not doing anything very well.

The proliferation of staff also enables ever more complex legislation. Every staffer wants to contribute something, so they work on lots of ideas. Often when Congress confronts a major issue, the staff puts many disparate pieces together in one massive bill. Everyone feels that the train is leaving the station, and this might be the last time that Congress addresses this topic for a long time. Often no single person understands the whole thing or thinks about it holistically. This process produces a tome that members cannot possibly read. Whatever understanding they have derives from brief summaries written by the same staffers who assembled the bill.

The income tax code illustrates the complexity of modern legislation quite nicely. People who have attempted to prepare their own tax returns can appreciate the need for simplicity. Whether Congress chooses to use the tax code as a means of redistributing wealth or encouraging investment, average citizens ought to be able to do their own returns. The same could be said for the campaign finance laws and numerous other areas of federal law.

As the complexity of bills increases, the influence of staff increases. These unelected staffers end up making decisions about details that elected members should be making, which ultimately undermines the democratic process.

As a thought experiment, imagine a Congress with no staff in which members do all their own legislating. That would necessarily limit the number of topics addressed and the complexity of the bills. No matter how great their talents, the 535 members simply could not do what they do now with more than 10,000 staffers. Members would actually have to make some tough choices about legislative priorities. One suspects that they would find that they could do without some of the superfluous things they have the staff doing now.

For example, members might think about eliminating commemorative bills. As noted in Chapter 6, over a third of the public laws that Congress passed in 2007-08 were purely honorary in nature. As the frozen food lobbyist told Rick Johnson, it gives members and lobbyists something to put in their newsletters. While they are relatively small projects individually, each one consumes a certain amount of time and energy that could be better directed to more meaningful matters. If they feel the need, members could use their publicly funded web sites to post bills that they would introduce but for the ban or post other material in which they express the same thought that otherwise would be in the bill.

While it is interesting to think about, members are not going to eliminate the whole staff. But if Congress implemented the budget ideas suggested in Chapter 12, members might actually cut back some of the staff and start drafting some of their own bills. Representatives did this until 1916 and senators until 1919. That would likely lead to fewer bills being introduced. Those that were introduced would likely be easier to understand. Those that were enacted would likely be easier for the public to understand.[3] At a minimum, fewer staff would mean that elected members, rather than unelected staff, would control the details.

If Congress chose to make these changes, members might actually have time to read the bills they are considering. Let's turn to that idea now.

Endnotes

See all endnote links at <www.TCNABC.com>.

1. See N.C. Gen.Stat. § 163-278.13B(c); Tex. Election Code § 253.034. Twenty-eight state legislatures have a full or partial ban on campaign contributions while they are in session. See "Limits on Contributions During the Legislative Session," NCSL.

2. *North Carolina Right to Life, Inc. v. Bartlett,* 168 F.3d 705 (4th Cir. 1999).

3. Again, this is no criticism of the professional legislative drafters that the Senate and House currently employ. They do what the members instruct them to do. It is not what they do—it is what their existence enables.

Chapter Fourteen

Reading Is Fundamental

"I love these members that get up and say, 'Read the bill!' Well, what good is reading the bill if it's a thousand pages and you don't have two days and two lawyers to find out what it means after you've read the bill?"

Rep. John Conyers, Jr.
On reading the 2010 health care reform bill[1]

"I don't think you want me to waste my time to read every page of the health care bill. You know why? It's statutory language. We hire experts."

Sen. Max Baucus
On reading the 2010 health care reform bill[2]

Congress has gotten into a lot of trouble with the public because members often do not understand the bills they are considering. As the quotes above make clear, even some of the key players did not read the health care reform bill passed in 2010. In the midst of the debate, Speaker Nancy Pelosi seemed to discourage the public from reading it. Speaking before a group of local government officials, she said: "But we have to pass the bill so that you can find out what is in it, away from the fog of the controversy."[3] Nor is this issue confined to Democrats. When Republicans controlled Congress, they too passed many complicated bills that few members had the time to read or understand.

Basic common sense dictates that members cannot make an informed choice about how to vote on bills if they have not read or understood them. But how can we get them to do that? Under the

current way of doing business, they do not seem to have any inclination to do so.

Congress could lighten its reading load by restricting the number of bills introduced. In the 110th Congress that met in 2007-08, representatives introduced 7,340 bills or about seventeen per member. Senators introduced 3,741 bills, or about thirty-seven per member.[4] Yet, only 460 of those 11,081 bills (about 4 percent) became law, and over a third of those were purely honorary in nature. Drafting and working on all of those bills consumes staff time and other resources. Given these figures, it sounds like Congress could probably make do with fewer introduced bills.

Both chambers could limit each member to introducing ten bills per Congress. Not all members would use their allocation, and they could be allowed to pass them to other members who may want to introduce more than ten bills. A monetary bonus could also be paid for not using the entire allocation. Having this kind of rule would force members to focus on the legislation that they really want to pass. It would also save the resources expended on all the other bills that are now introduced and quickly forgotten. Members could freely use their government web sites to post drafts on which they may want to seek public comment without using up their allocations.

Both chambers could also require that bills be drafted in plain English. As this book was being written, Congress enacted the "Plain Writing Act of 2010."[5] It required all executive branch agencies to use plain English in their documents. Sadly, Congress did not apply the same requirement to its documents. If it did, that would lighten the load for members.

As the quotes from Representative Conyers and Senator Baucus illustrate, members find current bill language dense and difficult to understand. If bills were drafted in clearer language, perhaps more members would read and understand them. If the bills then became law, the public might understand them better as well. Of the 460 public laws passed during 2007-08, seventeen were technical corrections bills that fixed drafting mistakes in prior laws—that Congress needed to pass so many of these bills illustrates the problems that complexity introduces.

The comments of Representative Conyers, Senator Baucus, and Speaker Pelosi also show that members do not read and understand bills because they are too long. The final version of the health care reform bill ran to over 2,400 pages in bill form.[6] To even contemplate reading through it numbs the mind. Its sheer length belies the notion that any single member actually read it or understood it. Yet bills of extreme length are increasingly common. The financial services reform bill passed in the summer of 2010 ran to more than 1,600 pages in bill form.[7] Republicans were equally guilty of this kind of excess when they ran Congress.

Both chambers could limit bills to a reasonable number of pages. One hundred pages seems like a reasonable number. If there were just a flat prohibition on the number of pages in introduced bills, members could game that requirement by adding amendments. Leaders could address this in a couple of ways. One would be to announce that they will not bring bills to the floor unless the bill, with its amendments, is less than one hundred pages. Another way would be to require separate votes for each one hundred pages. In either case, the point is to bring the proposal down to a digestible size so that members actually make an informed choice when they vote and can be held accountable for their votes.

Those requirements will make little difference unless the rules also require an adequate time to read the bills. House Republican leader John Boehner suggested during the 2010 midterm campaign that no bill be brought up until it had been available to members for seventy-two hours. That seems like a reasonable time. If it were enforced, no member could use lack of time as an excuse for not reading the bills.

All of these common sense reforms could easily be embodied in rules of the chamber or leadership policies. Getting members to actually read the bills and understand them is another matter entirely. It is not clear how either chamber could realistically enforce such a rule or policy. However, it could be made into campaign fodder. A party could

encourage its members to take a campaign pledge to read and under-stand every bill they vote on. It would be hard for an opponent not to make the same pledge. We would have to rely on the candidates' honor that they are actually doing so. But if they did not, they would certainly face embarrassing questions from the media when they broke it.

The changes suggested in this chapter are relatively easy to enact, but they would make a world of difference in how Congress operates. Had they been in effect, it is likely that we would have had a much sim-pler and easier to understand health care reform bill and that the pub-lic would be much happier with the product.

Endnotes

See all endnote links at <www.TCNABC.com>.

1. The video of this quote is available on YouTube, "John Conyers on Reading the Healthcare Bill."

2. The quote was reported in "Libby Residents Relate Gains, Drawbacks of As-bestos Aid," by Dan Testa, (Kalispell, MT) Flathead Beacon, August 24, 2010.

3. Her prepared remarks are available as "Pelosi Remarks at the 2010 Legislative Conference for National Association of Counties," Press Release from the Office of the Speaker of the House, March 9, 2010.

4. These figures do not include joint resolutions, concurrent resolutions, or sim-ple resolutions. For more on these types of legislation, see *Congressional Deskbook*, §§ 11.20, 11.30. For an explanation of how these numbers were derived, see Appen-dix A.

5. Pub. L. No. 111-274, 124 Stat. 2861 (2010). Prior to the passage of H.R. 946 (2010), efforts to get members of the executive branch to use plain English had gone on for a number of years, but they had been somewhat sporadic. See "A History of Plain Language in the United States Government (2004)," by Joanne Locke, Plain-Language.gov; President Clinton signed a memorandum encouraging the use of plain English in the executive branch in 1998, "Executive Memorandum of June 1, 1998—Plain Language in Government Writing," Federal Register Volume 63, Number 111, FR Doc No: 98-15700.

6. Patient Protection and Affordable Care Act, Pub. L. No. 111-148, 124 Stat. 119 (2010).

7. Dodd-Frank Wall Street Reform and Consumer Protection Act, Pub. L. No. 111-203, 124 Stat. 1376 (2010).

Chapter Fifteen

A Purpose-
Driven Minority

"One man with courage makes a majority."
Andrew Jackson

"It does not require a majority to prevail,
but rather an irate, tireless minority
keen to set brush fires in people's minds.
Samuel Adams

S erving in Congress as a member of the minority party is not fun. But worse yet, minority party status leaves members with no purpose. The majority party decides all the important questions.[1] As a minority party staffer described his status to me some years back: "All we do is sit around, twiddle our thumbs, and complain."

The majority party's leaders determine what bills will be debated on the floor and in committee. They also determine for the most part what amendments the minority party can offer on the floor. As a general rule, they do not bring up controversial bills that minority party members introduce. Thus, minority party members have little chance of ever getting their ideas enacted into law unless they are completely without controversy.

With no outlet for their legislative ambitions, minority party members turn their attention to winning back the majority in the next election.[2] They have little to gain from cooperating with majority party members on wise policymaking, and they generally do not. Remember that Rick Johnson learned this in his first few months in the Capitol. He quickly abandoned any idea of cooperating with the majority and focused almost exclusively on winning the majority in the next election.

This state of affairs disserves the public in several ways. Whatever

the size of the minority, some significant part of the public voted for, and is represented by, the minority party members. That part of the public has little say in the public policy process. For two years until the next election, they sit on the sidelines with little influence on what Congress will do.

It is a truism that elections have consequences, and they should. In a campaign, each party should run on an agenda. The winning party should have the opportunity to attempt to enact its agenda. This is not an argument for proportional representation, but the minority party should not be sent into exile. It ought to have some say in the process. Under the current way of doing business, it has little. That exacerbates partisan division in the Congress. That partisan division dissipates a lot of time and energy that might be better directed toward to more productive activity.

Leaving the minority largely powerless also leads to the enactment of policies primarily favored by the majority party instead of consensus options. Such policies tend to serve favored constituencies over the broader public interest. As discussed in Chapters 1, 2, and 11, the current campaign finance rules force members to please numerous constituencies in order to raise enough money to fund their reelection efforts. That need only worsens the majority party's desire to please its favored constituencies over the public as a whole.

Is there any realistic way out of this box? If the minority party controlled some part of the agenda, minority party members would take on some responsibility for governing and have some incentive to cooperate on the majority's priorities. They would have something to focus on other than the next election. In addition, it would set up a true policy competition between the parties, and the public should benefit from that competition. It is probably too much to ask to expect a majority party in either chamber to change the chamber's rules to implement this kind of change. Trying to write a rule to implement it is probably more trouble than it is worth.

However, another precedent shows how to accomplish this goal. In the House, most non-controversial bills are considered under a procedure known as suspension of the rules.[3] This procedure provides for a shortened debate and requires a two-thirds supermajority for passage. Over the years, the party leaders have maintained an informal agreement that 70 percent of the bills considered under this procedure will be majority party bills and 30 percent will be minority party bills.

This system has worked well under both Democratic and Republican majorities and caused little discord. The agreement is not part of the House rules, and it is not written down anywhere. The minority has no formal means of enforcing it, but theoretically at least, they could refuse to vote for suspension bills if the majority breached the agreement.

The party leaders in both chambers could strike a similar agreement on controversial bills. Most majority party members probably could not stomach 30 percent, but 10 percent might work. Alternatively, it could be a set number of bills—ten or fifteen. It might go something like this. The majority party leadership offers to let the minority party leadership put a certain number of its controversial bills on the agenda. This might apply to committees and the floor. Other rules would apply as now and the majority would not give up procedural control of the committee or the floor when these minority bills are considered. Because this agreement would not be a formal rule, its exact interpretation would be left to informal negotiation between party leaders both at the committee and chamber levels.

Under such an agreement, minority party members could see some of their ideas enacted into law. They would have an incentive to develop policies that could win at least some majority party support. Since the number of bills would be relatively small, the minority party would have to think carefully about which of its bills to offer. It would want to choose its best options to show voters that it could govern if elected.

But the more important question is, what is in it for the majority? Why agree to such a deal? Won't it just become a means to embarrass the majority? Not necessarily. It would transfer a small part of the responsibility for governing to the minority. Thus, it would take away mi-

nority party members' freedom to sit back and hurl bombs from the back benches. They would have to put up some real proposals or shut up. That can be useful to majority party members as they campaign for reelection.

It also sets up a market for trading votes between the majority and the minority. Under the current rules, the minority has little incentive to cooperate with the majority and give it victories. However, if minority party members could bring up some of their own bills, they would have an incentive to cooperate with the majority on some bills to get majority votes for their own bills. That increased cooperation could significantly benefit the majority. That trading market should move both sides' bills away from more partisan solutions and toward more consensus options.

A majority party would certainly worry that the minority would use such a system only to create embarrassing votes for the majority. That could be the case, but therein lies the beauty of having an informal agreement. If the minority abuses it, the majority can simply cancel it and return to the old system. That the agreement exists only at the sufferance of the majority goes a long way to discipline the minority to put serious proposals on the table.

Such a system may well have flaws that will not be exposed until it is tried. However, the leaders should give it a chance. If minority members no longer had the luxury of devoting all their energy to the next election, the majority members would benefit. Ultimately, the public would be better off if the interparty struggle became a true policy competition rather than the mindless political brawl that exists now.

Endnotes

See all endnote links at <www.TCNABC.com>.

1. This is more true in the House than in the Senate, but the principles discussed here apply to both.

2. For more on members' focus on elections, see *Persuading Congress*, Chapter 14.

3. See Rule XV, Clause 1, Rules of the House of Representatives.

Chapter Sixteen

The Committee on Repeals

"No government ever voluntarily reduces itself in size. Government programs, once launched, never disappear. Actually, a government bureau is the nearest thing to eternal life we'll ever see on this earth!"

Ronald Reagan

"Congress, the press, and the bureaucracy too often focus on how much money or effort is spent, rather than whether the money or effort actually achieves the announced goal."

Donald Rumsfeld

n Chapter 7, we looked at members' desire for accomplishments to propel their reelection bids. Almost always, they view an accomplishment as a new law, a new government program, or an addition to an existing one. Often, these accomplishments do not differ that much from already existing laws or programs, but the member can attach his name to them.

At the same time, the federal code is chock-full of outdated and obsolete statutes. The federal bureaucracy teems with programs that may have made some sense at the time they were passed, but that no longer serve any useful purpose. No rational person can look at them and seriously argue that we need every single one.

Sometimes these laws stay on the books because they benefit one favored interest group at the expense of the rest of the public. That constituency works hard to retain them. Other times, they stay simply

because of congressional inertia.[1] All of Congress's momentum runs in the direction of passing new laws rather than getting rid of old laws.

Congress could change that dynamic by creating a committee with jurisdiction extending only to bills that repeal existing laws. Its jurisdiction might also include rescissions of already appropriated funds.[2] The chair of this committee could not show any accomplishments other than repeals or rescissions. The creation of such a committee would to some extent impinge on the jurisdictions of other committees and they might oppose its creation.

Party leaders could mitigate that opposition by writing the rule creating a committee on repeals so that it gave a secondary referral to the committee with jurisdiction over the statute the law proposes to repeal. The key element, however, is that this secondary referral must limit the time for the second committee to act. If it does not act by the deadline, the rule would discharge the secondary committee from further consideration of the bill. Thus, if the secondary committee has a better solution to the problem, it can propose it. The party leaders can hash out the conflict after both committees have acted and before a final bill goes to the floor.

When the Republicans took over the House in 1995, they instituted a practice of setting time limits for secondary committees, and it continues in effect today.[3] It has eliminated the standoff that previously occurred when a bill fell within the jurisdiction of more than one committee. Before that change, either committee could bottle up a bill until it got its way. The deadline generally works to force the secondary committee to come to some form of compromise with the first committee. A new committee with jurisdiction over repeals and rescissions would represent a departure for the House. But the concept of the secondary referral with a time limitation has worked well and would not be new.

The Senate is another matter. It rarely refers bills to more than one committee.[4] However, instituting a secondary referral with a time limit might make it easier to create a committee on repeals.[5]

A committee on repeals might also have jurisdiction over a bill to create a sunset commission for federal government agencies. A sunset commission periodically reviews the activities of government agencies and makes recommendations as to whether the agency should continue in existence. Texas has such a statute. Its law provides a specific date on which each agency will go out of existence unless the Texas legislature renews it. As that date approaches, the Texas Sunset Advisory Commission conducts a thorough review of the agency's activities and makes recommendations to the legislature about it.[6] A sunset commission may or may not work at the federal level, but it would be a reasonable area of inquiry for a committee focused on repealing unnecessary laws.

A chair of this committee could only have accomplishments by working on repeal or rescission bills. That would create an incentive for him to look at laws and determine whether they were needed—not to create new laws. He could tout his accomplishments as saving money. He might not succeed in repealing a single law, but he would at least create some pressure for every other committee and every federal agency to justify the existence of their programs. Once that debate gets started, the other committees and the federal agencies themselves might find a few things that they can live without. At a minimum, this committee would counter the overwhelming momentum to create more government solutions to address every human problem.

Chairs of other committees will likely resist this idea, but the 2010 midterm elections showed deep public concern about the growth of government. It is an idea whose time has come.

Endnotes

See all endnote links at <www.TCNABC.com>.

1. For more on congressional inertia, see *Persuading Congress*, Chapter 19.

2. Sometimes Congress appropriates funds for a particular purpose and then they are not spent for one reason or another. This money then stays in the agency and is often spent for some other purpose with the approval of the congressional appropriators. The money is known as an unobligated balance and the process is known as reprogramming. For more on these matters, see *Congressional Deskbook*, § 9.140 Transfer and Reprogramming.

3. See Rule XII, Clause 2, Rules of the United States House of Representatives.

4. See Rule XVII, Paragraph 3, Rules of the United States Senate.

5. For more on how bills are referred to committees in the House and Senate, see *Congressional Deskbook*, § 8.30 Referral of Legislation to Committee.

6. For more information on the Texas process, see the commission's web site at: *<http://www.sunset.state.tx.us>*. Interestingly, several members from Texas have introduced bills to bring this concept to the federal government. See "Federal Sunset Act of 2009," H.R. 393, 111th Cong. (2009) (introduced by Rep. Kevin Brady); "Responsible Government Empowerment Act of 2009," H.R. 534, 111th Cong. (2009) (introduced by Rep. Randy Neugebauer); "Spending, Deficit, and Debt Control Act of 2009," H.R. 3964, 111th Cong. (2009) (introduced by Rep. Jeb Hensarling); and "United States Authorization and Sunset Commission Act of 2009," S. 926, 111th Cong. (2009) (introduced by Sen. John Cornyn).

Chapter Seventeen

Just Do It

*"If the present Congress errs in too much talking,
how can it be otherwise in a body to which the
people send one hundred and fifty lawyers,
whose trade it is to question everything,
yield nothing, and talk by the hour?"*

Thomas Jefferson

*"I served with General Washington in the Legislature
of Virginia... and... with Dr. Franklin in Congress.
I never heard either of them speak ten minutes
at a time, nor to any but the main point."*

Thomas Jefferson

Under current Senate rules, senators may debate bills without any time limit unless sixty senators vote to end debate.[1] If a senator wants to kill a bill, he may take advantage of this supermajority requirement and try to talk it to death. In the past, senators rarely filibustered, and the procedure was reserved for the most important issues.

In more recent years, Senate practice has allowed senators to stop bills merely by notifying party leaders that they intend to filibuster a bill if the majority leader calls it up. This practice is known as placing a hold on a bill. Currently, any senator can place a hold on any bill without making the hold public. In most instances, that is the end of the matter. The majority leader never moves to take up the matter simply because he does not want to expend the floor time to deal with the proposed filibuster.[2]

This state of affairs gives individual senators a lot of power. They can stop almost any bill that they do not like simply by placing a hold on it. Not surprisingly, the practice has proliferated. That proliferation leaves the Senate in a dysfunctional state much of the time. As a practical matter, proponents must have sixty votes to cut off debate to get anything with any degree of controversy passed.

Always frustrating for those in the majority, the threat of a filibuster serves as an important bulwark of minority rights. George Washington said that the Senate should serve as a saucer in which impassioned legislation from the House could be allowed to cool.[3] The filibuster and the sixty-vote supermajority requirement help it serve that function.

But today the situation has gotten out of hand. Individual senators frequently bring the Senate to a halt while exerting little effort. They use the secret hold far too often. On the other hand, the Senate requires a two-thirds supermajority (sixty-seven senators) to cut off debate on a change to its rules.[4] It is highly unlikely that sixty-seven senators will vote to reduce their power by changing the rules.[5] Nor should they. Minorities have to have some say.

Party leaders could change their practices to make it harder to mount a filibuster. A majority leader could easily eliminate the practice of secret holds. Currently, this is only an operating practice, and the Senate rules do not require it. Senator Ron Wyden has introduced a resolution that would write the elimination of holds into the Senate rules,[6] but the leaders could simply end the practice if they chose to. Ending the secrecy would go a long way to stop the overuse of the filibuster.

Party leaders could also change their practices by requiring senators who place holds on bills to actually stand on the floor and conduct the threatened filibuster. As noted above, this was the practice in years past, but it has faded away in recent times. Now the Senate rarely witnesses a senator conducting a true filibuster as Jimmy Stewart did in the film "Mr. Smith Goes to Washington." Party leaders could strengthen their hand further by making it known that if a senator places a hold on a bill, they intend to bring up the bill at the first opportunity and force the senator to begin his filibuster. That would force the disagreeing parties to negotiate rather than just to let the bill sit in limbo as frequently occurs now.

The Senate supermajority requirement provides the minority party with much-needed leverage to protect its rights. But both parties have overused it in recent years. Party leaders need to exert some discipline to see that senators use it more judiciously. They can do that without changing any of the Senate's current rules.

Unfortunately, the threat of a filibuster wreaks particular havoc on the lives of executive and judicial branch nominees. We consider that problem in the next chapter.

Endnotes

See all endnote links at <www.TCNABC.com>.

1. Rule XXII, Clause 2, Rules of the United States Senate. The same rule applies to amendments, resolutions, nominations, and other matters. For the sake of convenience, this chapter uses the term "bill" to encompass all of these matters.

The rule does not apply to budget reconciliation bills because Senate debate is limited to twenty hours. See *Congressional Deskbook*, § 9.110.

2. A hold is not a prerequisite to a filibuster. A Senator may simply begin a filibuster when a bill is called up without having previously placed a hold on it. For more on these topics, see *Congressional Deskbook*, §§ 8.190, 8.200, 8.210, 8.230.

3. For more on how the founders viewed the role of the Senate, see Federalist Papers No. 63.

4. See Rule XXII, Paragraph 2, Rules of the United States Senate. During 2010, the Senate Rules Committee held a series of hearings to examine the filibuster and related rules and practices. These hearings are available on the committee's web site.

5. Some contend that a newly elected Senate could rewrite its rules by majority vote. Reasonable people can reach different conclusions on that point, but it is unlikely to happen in practice.

6. See S. Res. 502, A resolution eliminating secret Senate holds (111th Congress) (2010).

Chapter Eighteen

Hurry Up and Wait

"Nominee. A modest gentleman shrinking from the distinction of private life and diligently seeking the honorable obscurity of public office."

Ambrose Bierce, *The Devil's Dictionary*

"A deadline is negative inspiration. Still, it's better than no inspiration at all."

Rita Mae Brown

According to the 2008 Plum Book, the executive branch has 1,141 jobs that require Senate confirmation.[1] These jobs range from Cabinet Secretaries to local United States attorneys to many lesser posts. They tend to turn over fairly frequently with a typical tenure being two or three years. In addition, Congress has authorized 866 federal judgeships, each of which requires Senate confirmation.[2] Federal judges are appointed for life, but at any given time, dozens of judgeships are vacant because of deaths, retirements, and resignations.

Under current practice, the potential nominee seeking any of these jobs faces a lengthy and arduous process from initial interest to swearing in. In most cases, he must begin by campaigning for the presidential nomination against several competitors. Once the President settles on a nominee, he must then go through an extensive vetting process with the White House. This involves filling out lots of paperwork about personal matters, undergoing background checks, and having candid conversations with White House lawyers about any flaws in his background. Assuming he passes all those checks, his nomination gets sent up to the Senate and referred to the committee of jurisdiction.

Then a similar process begins again. The nominee must fill out a whole new mountain of paperwork for the Senate committee.[3] Typically, the committee's questionnaire will overlap with the White House's, but it will not be identical.

Once the nominee completes the paperwork, he may be expected to pay courtesy visits on the senators on the committee. Then he sits and waits for the committee to hold a hearing on his nomination. That may take months even if no senator has any objection to his confirmation. The wait may occur for all sorts of reasons that have nothing to do with the nominee. Or it may occur because one senator has some objection to him. Often, the nominee may not even know why his nomination is not moving.

Whenever the committee decides to move forward on the nomination, the nominee must appear before the committee for a formal hearing. If there is no objection to the nominee, the hearing may be perfunctory. If a senator objects to the nominee, then the senator may grill him in the hearing. Usually, once a committee chair holds a hearing, the committee moves to report out the nomination shortly thereafter assuming the hearing has not raised any new questions.

Once a nomination clears the relevant committee, it moves to the Senate calendar. If there is no controversy and the nomination is an important one, the Senate may take it up in a matter of days. However, if there is controversy or it is not particularly important, it may sit on the calendar for weeks or months before it gets attention. A senator may hold it up because he has some unrelated problem with the agency in which the nominee would serve. Typically, the Senate clears its calendar of nominations just before it goes home for a recess.

One example of this process in action occurred in September 2010. Senator Mary Landrieu of Louisiana placed a hold on the nomination of Jack Lew to be director of the Office Management and Budget. Senator Landrieu had no problem with Mr. Lew, but she was unhappy about the Obama administration's moratorium on oil drilling in the Gulf of Mexico in the aftermath of the British Petroleum oil spill.[4] Mr. Lew had nothing to do with the moratorium. But nonetheless, his nomination did not move. Whatever its merits, the drilling moratorium had grave economic consequences for Senator Landrieu's state, and she was no doubt sincere in her efforts to get it lifted.

On the other hand, the job to which President Obama has nominated Mr. Lew is an important one that needs to be filled. On October 12, 2010, the Obama administration lifted the moratorium in hopes of getting the hold lifted. Senator Landrieu then announced that she would maintain her hold on Mr. Lew until she had a chance to review how things developed.[5] That Senator Landrieu would take Mr. Lew as the hostage in this case is particularly ironic—he had previously held the same position in the Clinton administration.

The current confirmation process does not serve the public's interest for at least two reasons. Because of its length, many jobs go vacant for months at the time. That was certainly the case with Mr. Lew's nomination. His predecessor left in June 2010. As of mid-November 2010, he was still not confirmed. Many capable civil servants fill in as temporary or "acting" office holders, but it is always better to have a fully empowered, Senate-confirmed person at the helm.

Aside from that, the burdensomeness of the process discourages qualified candidates from seeking these jobs. While it is ongoing, the nominee must put his life on hold. If, for example, he is a practicing lawyer, he must take care not to take on any new clients that might cause controversy. He cannot make any major changes to his financial situation for fear of hurting his nomination. In Mr. Lew's case, he held a senior job in the State Department while his nomination was before the Senate. During that time, he may have felt inhibited him from taking actions in that job that he otherwise would have because of the pendency of his nomination.

In short, a potential nominee must want the job badly to submit to this process. That may not be the best thing for the job or the country. It would make more sense to design a process that actually tests the nominee's qualifications rather than to have the endurance contest that now prevails.

Unfortunately, the Senate probably will not change its basic pro-

cedures for nominations. The ability to hold them up for unrelated reasons gives senators too much leverage over the executive branch. The Lew episode provides a good example. Senator Landrieu wanted to change the administration's policy on the drilling moratorium, and she used the tools she had at hand. Senators will not give up those tools easily. Because Senate rules changes require a two-thirds supermajority, it is unlikely that any will occur in this area in the foreseeable future.[6]

However, a determined Senate leadership could change its practices in some ways that will improve the situation. A majority and minority leader could together encourage each of the committees to review the number of executive branch positions under their jurisdiction that require Senate confirmation and look for those that can be pared back. We could probably get by just fine with fewer than a thousand. If fewer such positions required confirmation, fewer people would have to go through this process. From the Senate's perspective, it could devote more time to those that remain.

Candidates who have put forth the effort to get their nominations before the Senate deserve a vote.[7] The public deserves to have the jobs filled. For both those reasons, the committees ought to have some reasonable deadline by which they must act.

That could realistically happen. A majority leader could institute a policy that, after a nominee's full information has been before a committee for 90 or 120 days, he will move to discharge it if the committee has not acted.[8] The leader could do this once a month for all committees. A majority leader could make exceptions if a committee chair shows good cause.

But such a policy would tilt the presumption in favor of forward motion rather than standstill. It would advance a lot of non-controversial nominees who get stuck simply because the relevant committee's attention is elsewhere. The majority leader could then make it his policy to move the confirmations of those nominees a week later if the nominations have no further problems. That would give senators adequate time to raise any objections they might have and allow them to keep their leverage on nominations with true controversy.

Some might argue that this will lead to inadequate vetting of candidates. However, having reasonable deadlines should not reduce the amount of vetting that occurs. It should simply make it happen more promptly. Even if that argument were valid, the benefits of getting jobs filled and encouraging qualified candidates to serve would greatly outweigh the damage of a few bad nominees getting confirmed.

If the jobs are important enough to require Senate confirmation, then they are important enough to require Senate votes within a reasonable amount of time. The process should serve to cull unqualified candidates without unduly burdening qualified ones. It should also get the jobs filled promptly. The current process does neither. It culls qualified candidates who do not want to submit to the process, and it leaves the jobs unfilled for months. The Senate, the President, the nominees, and the public all deserve better.

Endnotes

See all endnote links at <www.TCNABC.com>.

1. Just after each presidential election, Congress publishes a document entitled "United States Government Policy and Supporting Positions" that enumerates the various non-civil service jobs in the executive branch. This document is commonly known as the Plum Book, both because of the color of its cover and its contents. The most recent version is available online at: <*www.gpoaccess.gov/plumbook/*>.

2. For more information on the federal judiciary, see the web site of the Federal Judicial Center: <*www.fjc.gov*>.

3. For example, the 202-page questionnaire filled out by Supreme Court Justice Elena Kagan can be viewed on Scribd, "ElenaKagan-PublicQuestionnaire."

4. Senator Landrieu's statements on this matter are available online: "Landrieu Maintains Hold on OMB Nominee," Press Release, September 29, 2010, and letter from Senator Landrieu to Majority Leader Harry Reid, September 23, 2010.

5. "Landrieu Responds to Obama Administration Decision to Lift Deepwater Drilling Moratorium," Press Release, October 12, 2010.

6. See Rule XXII, Paragraph 2, Rules of the United States Senate.

7. In the debates over ratification of the Constitution, the founders did not seem to contemplate the possibility of the interminable delays inherent in today's confirmation process. See Federalist Papers No. 76. They seemed to think that the threat to the President's nominees would be defeat in a confirmation vote—not death by never having a vote.

8. See Rule XVII, Paragraph 4, Rules of the United States Senate.

Chapter Nineteen

Be It Ever So Humble

*"A small body of determined spirits fired
by an unquenchable faith in their mission
can alter the course of history."*

Mohandas Gandhi

*"It is with books as with men:
a very small number play a great part,
the rest are lost in the multitude."*

Francois Marie Arouet (better known as Voltaire)

The House of Representatives currently consists of 435 members representing the fifty states.[1] Congress sets this number by statute, and no particular rationale justifies 435 as opposed to 400 or 470. The Constitution provided for a House composed of sixty-five members until the first census was taken.[2] From that time until 1911, Congress regularly increased the number as the country added new states and more population.[3] In 1911, Congress passed a law capping the number of House members at 435, and it has remained there since that time.[4]

According to the 1910 census, the total U.S. population was just over 100 million.[5] Currently, the total U.S. population is more than three times that number, or about 310 million.[6] So representatives now have on average about three times more constituents than they did in 1911 when Congress set the number.

Some believe that this leads to a diminution of democracy. Indeed, some members of Congress have introduced legislation to set up a commission to study whether the number of representatives ought to be increased.[7] But these arguments overlook the practicalities.

If the number of representatives had grown three times, we would now have a House consisting of 1,305 members. That number approximates the number of delegates to the national political conventions. Try to picture one of those bodies acting to pass laws like Congress does. As a purely practical matter, it is hard to see how such a large body could function at all. The increased cost alone would be astronomical.

Let's assume that Congress increased the number of representatives to 1,305. Those representatives would get elected in districts with populations that were about one-third of their current districts. The number would be about 240,000 people, as opposed to the current number of around 700,000. With those narrower constituencies, more members with extreme views on both ends of the spectrum would likely be elected. As discussed in Chapter 6, more members driven by reelection concerns would dream up more and more micro-problems that Congress would need to address. Almost any organized interest—no matter how small—could find some member to champion its cause.[8] The House would quickly reach the point at which it could not govern itself, much less the rest of the country.

But what if Congress changed the number in the other direction? A smaller House would have some significant benefits. The cost of running the House would certainly be lower. That is a positive, but it is not enough to change our well-worn ways on this issue.

The real question is whether we would actually get better legislation. As the number of representatives drops, the constituencies they represent get larger. As their constituencies get larger, their policy positions must move to the middle to win elections. With more members in the middle, the House might reach consensus on more policies. At a minimum, it ought to be less polarized. A smaller number would also allow members to get to know each other better and form personal relationships across the aisle. That too might lead to less polarization.

The founders certainly intended the House of Representatives to be the part of the new government that would be closest to the people.[9] One can plausibly argue that larger constituencies would mean that representatives would get ever farther away from the people. Certainly, that would have been true during the horse-and-buggy days of the late 18th century.

In today's world of incredible technology and instant round-the-world communication, it is less true. For example, a member can sit in his office in Washington and conduct a telephone town hall directly with thousands of constituents who sit in the privacy of their own homes. That is probably as close as the vast majority of average citizens ever get to their members today. Citizens would certainly give up something in closeness if the average district went from 700,000 people to 1 million people. But it would be worth it if Congress produced legislation that was more in line with what the public wants.

Another issue that would arise from a smaller House would be the effect on minority representation. Let me say that I am no expert on the Voting Rights Act, and I would not advocate for a change that would violate it. However, if Congress lowered the number of representatives, everything could be done on a proportional basis. Thus, while the absolute number of majority-minority districts might go down, the ratio of majority-minority districts to the total number of seats could remain the same. The election of an African-American President and the shrinking number of non-Hispanic whites as a percentage of the total population ought to lessen these concerns if the change were made 20 years in the future.[10]

How realistic is this idea? In the short run, it is probably not very realistic. No representative will vote for a smaller House if he sees any possibility that it would eliminate his seat, and it would necessarily eliminate some seats. To have any chance of passing, such a change would have to be made ten or twenty years in advance, to take effect after a future census. That way, all interested parties would have plenty of time to adjust their career expectations. Members do that now within their state delegations as each decennial reapportionment and redistricting process approaches.[11]

If such a law were passed to take effect after a future census, it

might not last. As the time to reduce the House approached, the pressure would be strong to increase the number again. Despite that danger, this is a debate worth having.

Endnotes

See all endnote links at <www.TCNABC.com>.

1. The District of Columbia and five U.S. territories also elect delegates to the House. These delegates can vote in committees, but not on the floor.

2. U.S. Const. art. I, § 2, cl. 3.

3. See the web site of the Clerk of the House for more detailed information on this growth. Interestingly, during the debates on the Constitution, there was great concern that Congress would not increase the number of representatives as the population increased. See Federalist Papers Nos. 55, 56, and 58.

4. Pub. L. No. 62-5, §§ 1-2, 37 Stat. 13-14 (1911).

5. See Thirteenth Census of the United States: 1910, Chapter 1: Number and Distribution of Inhabitants.

6. See U.S. & World Population Clocks, U.S. Census Bureau.

7. See H.R. 3972, the "Congress 2014 Commission Act," 111th Congress (2010).

8. For more on members championing causes, see *Persuading Congress*, Chapter 30.

9. See Federalist Papers Nos. 52, 53, and 57.

10. The United States Census Bureau projects that minorities will make up a majority of the U.S. population by 2042. See "An Older and More Diverse Nation by Midcentury," Press Release, U.S. Census Bureau, August 14, 2008.

11. Most states allow their state legislatures to redraw the lines while a few use commissions of various sorts. If there were fewer seats in the House, the task would be easier. For more on reapportionment and redistricting, see *Congressional Deskbook*, §§ 2.10, 2.13.

Chapter Twenty

Other People's Money

*"That most delicious of all privileges—
spending other people's money."*

John Randolph of Roanoke

*"I love deadlines. I like the whooshing
sound they make as they fly by."*

Douglas Adams, British Comic

Voters view Congress poorly in part because it overspends. Congress acts as if the federal treasury contains an infinite supply of money. This behavior has continued whether Democrats or Republicans have controlled the levers of power. It cannot continue indefinitely, and voters realize that now more than ever. That, in part, led to the dramatic results in the 2010 midterm elections.

Under Article I, Section 7 of the Constitution, bills to raise revenue must originate in the House. By tradition, the House has interpreted this provision to extend to both taxing and spending bills. The Senate must still concur in spending bills, but the House tends to take the lead on them.

As currently practiced, the congressional spending process produces no discipline at all. Theoretically, the Congressional Budget Act requires Congress to produce an overall budget each year, to spend in accordance with that budget, and to achieve all of that on a tight time schedule.[1] In practice, Congress rarely passes a budget resolution in both chambers. Even if it does, that budget usually only purports to limit spending on discretionary programs.[2] When Congress does manage to pass a budget, it frequently uses various procedural tactics to allow spending beyond the budget.[3]

Some have suggested that Congress move to a two-year budgeting process.[4] That would certainly be a good start. The chaotic process that Congress uses now for one year barely finishes before the next year's process begins. Members have little, if any, time to review spending and see whether it has achieved its stated goals. This headlong rush can hardly lead to efficient government spending. Anything that encourages longer-term thinking can only help.

When it comes to the actual spending bills, Congress theoretically enacts twelve of them each year. Each of the twelve bills funds a number of government agencies. In practice, however, Congress only rarely passes all twelve of them in a given year. Most often, some or all of them are rolled into one large omnibus spending bill at the end of the year. That bill usually takes up hundreds or thousands of pages. This haphazard budgeting process only encourages overspending by avoiding any true scrutiny of where the money goes.[5]

Another step toward reining in overspending would be to set strict deadlines and tight spending caps in the House. A determined Speaker and Majority Leader could simply announce that the Appropriations Committee must report each of the twelve bills by a certain date and with an amount of spending within the cap for the bill. If the committee does not meet those requirements, the leaders will not bring up that bill in the House.

Congress would still need to pass funding for that part of the government. To do so, the leaders could insist on a so-called continuing resolution for the entire upcoming fiscal year in lieu of the bill.[6] If enforced, this system would force the House appropriators to get their work done on a timely basis. Then the leaders would have to follow through by bringing up the bills in the House on a timely basis.

Even if the House operated under such a system and got all twelve spending bills passed early, the Senate must still act on them. The House cannot force the Senate to act. But it can prevent the Senate from initiating them. Again, determined House leadership could set a schedule in consultation with the Senate leadership and set deadlines and spending caps. If the Senate does not meet its deadlines and caps, the House leadership can refuse to pass anything other than a continuing resolution for the part of the government covered by each bill.

Another area that needs attention is earmark spending. Defining an earmark is to some extent in the eye of the beholder. However, generally speaking, most people think of an earmark as an instance in which Congress designates money in a spending bill for a particular local project outside of any executive branch process. In other words, Congress dictates that the executive branch will spend money on the project regardless of any competitive process set out in general law.[7]

In theory, earmarks need not waste money. Members have argued that they know better than the executive branch how to spend money in their districts. That may well be true. In addition, earmarks comprise only a small percentage of all discretionary spending. But in recent years, earmarks have grown and grown. The pursuit of earmarks consumes a lot of time and resources both for members and for the outside groups that seek them. They often contribute to a public perception of congressional corruption as well.

Most problematic, however, is the competitive race to the bottom that they cause. If one member tries to get an earmark for his district, then all others must do so or risk being accused of not serving their district well. The more earmarks any one member gets, the more it creates pressure for others to get them. That increases the overall pressure to spend as if there is no tomorrow.

Getting rid of earmarks will again require determined leadership. The leaders of the House and Senate can announce a policy that they will not bring up spending bills that contain them. So long as they enforce that policy equally for everyone, it can work. It would allow members and staff to spend their time on other matters. It would relieve them of having to decide among the many worthy groups who want earmarks. Members could simply point to the policy and say that there is nothing they can do. They would no longer have to worry about a campaign charge that they are ineffective for not getting any earmarks. At the same time, groups could stop spending money trying to get them.

All of the solutions proposed so far go only to discretionary spend-

ing, a small part of our overall spending problem. Ever-expanding entitlement programs like Social Security, Medicare, and Medicaid make up by far the greatest part of it. As noted in Chapter 9, we cannot sustain any of them indefinitely as they exist under current law. The good news is that a variety of solutions can put them back on solid footing. The bad news is that Congress has not enacted any of these solutions and probably will not in the foreseeable future.

This problem goes beyond congressional procedure or rules—it is a matter of political will. Most members of Congress do not want to seriously address the entitlement programs. It is too easy for political opponents to demagogue the issue to a member's disadvantage. At the same time, it is too hard to enact solutions.

This book has no magic solution to this problem. However, it does offer more general solutions that could lead to a resolution of these issues. The solution offered in Chapter 10—to make serving in Congress a part-time job that members do not typically hold for life—could help. If members cared less about getting reelected and more about solving problems, they could potentially work more seriously on the entitlement issue.

Likewise, the solution offered in Chapter 15—to allow the minority to bring up a limited number of its bills during a session—might also change the dynamic of the entitlement issue. If a majority party could invite the minority to put up or shut up on the issue in a real way, then that might make it harder for a minority party to demagogue the issue.

We will not truly know until Congress tries these solutions. We do know that we cannot continue to spend the way we do now.

Endnotes

See all endnote links at <www.TCNABC.com>.

1. Pub. L. No. 93-344, 88 Stat. 297 (1974) (codified at 2 U.S.C. §§ 601–688).

2. Discretionary programs are those that Congress funds on a yearly basis (most government agencies, for example) as distinguished from non-discretionary entitlement programs like Social Security, Medicare, and Medicaid, under which benefits must be paid to anyone who meets the requirements of the law.

3. For more on the congressional budget process, see *Congressional Deskbook*, Chapter 9, "Federal Budget Process," and *Lobbying and Advocacy*, §§ 4.10-4.14.

4. See, for example, the "Biennial Budgeting and Appropriations Act," S. 169, 111th Cong. (2009).

5. Because such large spending bills become "must pass" items, all sorts of other mischievous provisions get inserted into them in the middle of the night. That is another reason to discourage them.

6. A continuing resolution provides for temporary spending at last year's level when Congress cannot pass a spending bill. They are often used as stopgap measures when a new fiscal year begins and Congress has not passed the necessary spending bills.

7. For more on earmarks, see *Lobbying and Advocacy*, §§ 4.29, 4.30.

Chapter Twenty-One

Conclusion—
Solutions, Solutions
Everywhere, But...

This book ends where it began. Congress does not work well. It produces results that are not what the public wants or needs. Like other human beings, members of Congress respond to incentives, and the incentives that Congress has set up for itself drive members to bad results. The 2010 midterm election results show that the public wants change. The new look of the 112th Congress provides a perfect opportunity for both chambers to rethink their ways.

Can all the changes discussed above actually happen in real life? Probably not. But some of them can. It is up to the members to decide which, if any, they will implement. Some of the ideas are new and some are old. Some are easy to do and some are hard. Some have been suggested by others, and some have not.

No one idea set forth in this book will cause the pillars of the Capitol to shake. But taken as a whole, they suggest how Congress can change its ways so that we can lift our country out of its current state. The ideas offered here are intended to provoke thought and sketch a vision of what that change could look like. If this book leads members and the public to take a good, hard look at the ways of Congress, it will have served its purpose. If we change the incentives, we can change the results.

Appendices

A. How the Figures for
   Numbers of Laws and Bills
   Used in This Book Were Derived

B. Declaration of Independence

C. U.S. Constitution
   and Amendments

Appendix A

How the Figures for Numbers of Laws and Bills Used in This Book Were Derived

In Chapters 6 and 14, this book gave some statistics about various laws that were passed and bills that were introduced in the 110th Congress that sat in 2007-08. These figures were derived from Thomas, a massive public database of legislative materials that the Library of Congress maintains. Thomas is available at: <*http://thomas.gov*>.

With respect to the various types of laws that the 110th Congress passed, the author identified the numbers of laws in each of the categories from a printout of all 460 public laws from Thomas. Most of the judgments are clear-cut, but a few are subject to interpretation. Thus, someone else performing the same count might come up with slightly different numbers, but they would not differ enough to alter the basic points that the book makes.

With respect to the total number of bills introduced, the author simply called up all the introduced bills on Thomas and took its number as the total.

Appendix B
Declaration of Independence

IN CONGRESS, July 4, 1776.

The unanimous Declaration of the thirteen united States of America,

When in the Course of human events, it becomes necessary for one people to dissolve the political bands which have connected them with another, and to assume among the powers of the earth, the separate and equal station to which the Laws of Nature and of Nature's God entitle them, a decent respect to the opinions of mankind requires that they should declare the causes which impel them to the separation.

We hold these truths to be self-evident, that all men are created equal, that they are endowed by their Creator with certain unalienable Rights, that among these are Life, Liberty and the pursuit of Happiness.—That to secure these rights, Governments are instituted among Men, deriving their just powers from the consent of the governed,—That whenever any Form of Government becomes destructive of these ends, it is the Right of the People to alter or to abolish it, and to institute new Government, laying its foundation on such principles and organizing its powers in such form, as to them shall seem most likely to effect their Safety and Happiness. Prudence, indeed, will dictate that Governments long established should not be changed for light and transient causes; and accordingly all experience hath shewn, that mankind are more disposed to suffer, while evils are sufferable, than to right themselves by abolishing the forms to which they are accustomed. But when a long train of abuses and usurpations, pursuing invariably the same Object evinces a design to reduce them under absolute Despotism, it is their right, it is their duty, to throw off such Government, and to provide new Guards for their future security.—Such has been the patient sufferance of these Colonies; and such is now the necessity which constrains them to alter their former Systems of Government. The history of the present King of Great Britain is a history of repeated injuries and usurpations, all having in direct object the establishment of an absolute Tyranny over these States. To prove this, let Facts be submitted to a candid world.

He has refused his Assent to Laws, the most wholesome and necessary for the public good.

He has forbidden his Governors to pass Laws of immediate and pressing importance, unless suspended in their operation till his Assent should be obtained; and when so suspended, he has utterly neglected to attend to them.

He has refused to pass other Laws for the accommodation of large districts of people, unless those people would relinquish the right of Representation in the Legislature, a right inestimable to them and formidable to tyrants only.

He has called together legislative bodies at places unusual, uncomfortable, and distant from the depository of their public Records, for the sole purpose of fatiguing them into compliance with his measures.

He has dissolved Representative Houses repeatedly, for opposing with manly firmness his invasions on the rights of the people.

He has refused for a long time, after such dissolutions, to cause others to be elected; whereby the Legislative powers, incapable of Annihilation, have returned to the People at large for their exercise; the State remaining in the mean time exposed to all the dangers of invasion from without, and convulsions within.

He has endeavoured to prevent the population of these States; for that purpose obstructing the Laws for Naturalization of Foreigners; refusing to pass others to encourage their migrations hither, and raising the conditions of new Appropriations of Lands.

He has obstructed the Administration of Justice, by refusing his Assent to Laws for establishing Judiciary powers.

He has made Judges dependent on his Will alone, for the tenure of their offices, and the amount and payment of their salaries.

He has erected a multitude of New Offices, and sent hither swarms of Officers to harrass our people, and eat out their substance.

He has kept among us, in times of peace, Standing Armies without the Consent of our legislatures.

He has affected to render the Military independent of and superior to the Civil power.

He has combined with others to subject us to a jurisdiction foreign to our constitution, and unacknowledged by our laws; giving his Assent to their Acts of pretended Legislation:

For Quartering large bodies of armed troops among us:

For protecting them, by a mock Trial, from punishment for any Murders which they should commit on the Inhabitants of these States:

For cutting off our Trade with all parts of the world:

For imposing Taxes on us without our Consent:

For depriving us in many cases, of the benefits of Trial by Jury:

For transporting us beyond Seas to be tried for pretended offences

For abolishing the free System of English Laws in a neighbouring Province, establishing therein an Arbitrary government, and enlarging its Boundaries so as to render it at once an example and fit instrument for introducing the same absolute rule into these Colonies:

For taking away our Charters, abolishing our most valuable Laws, and altering fundamentally the Forms of our Governments:

For suspending our own Legislatures, and declaring themselves invested with power to legislate for us in all cases whatsoever.

He has abdicated Government here, by declaring us out of his Protection and waging War against us.

He has plundered our seas, ravaged our Coasts, burnt our towns, and destroyed the lives of our people.

He is at this time transporting large Armies of foreign Mercenaries to compleat the works of death, desolation and tyranny, already begun with circumstances of Cruelty & perfidy scarcely paralleled in the most barbarous ages, and totally unworthy the Head of a civilized nation.

He has constrained our fellow Citizens taken Captive on the high Seas to bear Arms against their Country, to become the executioners of their friends and Brethren, or to fall themselves by their Hands.

He has excited domestic insurrections amongst us, and has endeavoured to bring on the inhabitants of our frontiers, the merciless Indian Savages, whose known rule of warfare, is an undistinguished destruction of all ages, sexes and conditions.

In every stage of these Oppressions We have Petitioned for Redress in the most humble terms: Our repeated Petitions have been answered only by repeated injury. A Prince whose character is thus marked by every act which may define a Tyrant, is unfit to be the ruler of a free people.

Nor have We been wanting in attentions to our Brittish brethren. We have warned them from time to time of attempts by their legislature to extend an unwarrantable jurisdiction over us. We have reminded them of the circumstances of our emigration and settlement here. We have appealed to their native justice and magnanimity, and we have conjured them by the ties of our common kindred to disavow these usurpations, which, would inevitably interrupt our connections and correspondence. They too have been deaf to the voice of justice and of consanguinity. We must, therefore, acquiesce in the necessity, which denounces our Separation, and hold them, as we hold the rest of mankind, Enemies in War, in Peace Friends.

We, therefore, the Representatives of the united States of America, in General Congress, Assembled, appealing to the Supreme Judge of the world for the rectitude of our intentions, do, in the Name, and by Authority of the good People of these Colonies, solemnly publish and declare, That these United Colonies are, and of Right ought to be Free and Independent States; that they are Absolved from all Allegiance to the British Crown, and that all political connection between them and the State of Great Britain, is and ought to be totally dissolved; and that as Free and Independent States, they have full Power to levy War, conclude Peace, contract Alliances, establish Commerce, and to do all other Acts and Things which Independent States may of right do. And for the support of this Declaration, with a firm reliance on the protection of divine Providence, we mutually pledge to each other our Lives, our Fortunes and our sacred Honor.

Georgia
Button Gwinnett
Lyman Hall
George Walton

North Carolina
William Hooper
Joseph Hewes
John Penn

South Carolina
Edward Rutledge
Thomas Heyward, Jr.
Thomas Lynch, Jr.
Arthur Middleton

Massachusetts
John Hancock

Maryland
Samuel Chase
William Paca
Thomas Stone
Charles Carroll
of Carrollton

Virginia
George Wythe
Richard Henry Lee
Thomas Jefferson
Benjamin Harrison
Thomas Nelson, Jr.
Francis Lightfoot Lee
Carter Braxton

Pennsylvania
Robert Morris
Benjamin Rush
Benjamin Franklin
John Morton
George Clymer
James Smith
George Taylor
James Wilson
George Ross

Delaware
Caesar Rodney
George Read
Thomas McKean

New York
William Floyd
Philip Livingston
Francis Lewis
Lewis Morris

New Jersey
Richard Stockton
John Witherspoon
Francis Hopkinson
John Hart
Abraham Clark

New Hampshire
Josiah Bartlett
William Whipple

Massachusetts
Samuel Adams
John Adams
Robert Treat Paine
Elbridge Gerry

Rhode Island
Stephen Hopkins
William Ellery

Connecticut
Roger Sherman
Samuel Huntington
William Williams
Oliver Wolcott

New Hampshire
Matthew Thornton

Appendix C
The Constitution
of the United States

We the People of the United States, in Order to form a more perfect Union, establish Justice, insure domestic Tranquility, provide for the common defence, promote the general Welfare, and secure the Blessings of Liberty to ourselves and our Posterity, do ordain and establish this Constitution for the United States of America.

Article. I.

Section. 1.

All legislative Powers herein granted shall be vested in a Congress of the United States, which shall consist of a Senate and House of Representatives.

Section. 2.

The House of Representatives shall be composed of Members chosen every second Year by the People of the several States, and the Electors in each State shall have the Qualifications requisite for Electors of the most numerous Branch of the State Legislature.

No Person shall be a Representative who shall not have attained to the Age of twenty five Years, and been seven Years a Citizen of the United States, and who shall not, when elected, be an Inhabitant of that State in which he shall be chosen.

Representatives and direct Taxes shall be apportioned among the several States which may be included within this Union, according to their respective Numbers, which shall be determined by adding to the whole Number of free Persons, including those bound to Service for a Term of Years, and excluding Indians not taxed, three fifths of all other Persons. The actual Enumeration shall be made within three Years after the first Meeting of the Congress of the United States, and within every subsequent Term of ten Years, in such Manner as they shall by Law direct. The Number of Representatives shall not exceed one for every thirty Thousand, but each State shall have at Least one Representative; and

until such enumeration shall be made, the State of New Hampshire shall be entitled to chuse three, Massachusetts eight, Rhode-Island and Providence Plantations one, Connecticut five, New-York six, New Jersey four, Pennsylvania eight, Delaware one, Maryland six, Virginia ten, North Carolina five, South Carolina five, and Georgia three.

When vacancies happen in the Representation from any State, the Executive Authority thereof shall issue Writs of Election to fill such Vacancies.

The House of Representatives shall chuse their Speaker and other Officers; and shall have the sole Power of Impeachment.

Section. 3.

The Senate of the United States shall be composed of two Senators from each State, chosen by the Legislature thereof for six Years; and each Senator shall have one Vote.

Immediately after they shall be assembled in Consequence of the first Election, they shall be divided as equally as may be into three Classes. The Seats of the Senators of the first Class shall be vacated at the Expiration of the second Year, of the second Class at the Expiration of the fourth Year, and of the third Class at the Expiration of the sixth Year, so that one third may be chosen every second Year; and if Vacancies happen by Resignation, or otherwise, during the Recess of the Legislature of any State, the Executive thereof may make temporary Appointments until the next Meeting of the Legislature, which shall then fill such Vacancies.

No Person shall be a Senator who shall not have attained to the Age of thirty Years, and been nine Years a Citizen of the United States, and who shall not, when elected, be an Inhabitant of that State for which he shall be chosen.

The Vice President of the United States shall be President of the Senate, but shall have no Vote, unless they be equally divided.

The Senate shall chuse their other Officers, and also a President pro tempore, in the Absence of the Vice President, or when he shall exercise the Office of President of the United States.

The Senate shall have the sole Power to try all Impeachments. When sitting for that Purpose, they shall be on Oath or Affirmation. When the President of the United States is tried, the Chief Justice shall preside: And no Person shall be convicted without the Concurrence of two thirds of the Members present.

Judgment in Cases of Impeachment shall not extend further than to removal from Office, and disqualification to hold and enjoy any Office of honor, Trust or Profit under the United States: but the Party convicted shall nevertheless be liable and subject to Indictment, Trial, Judgment and Punishment, according to Law.

Section. 4.

The Times, Places and Manner of holding Elections for Senators and Representatives, shall be prescribed in each State by the Legislature thereof; but the Congress may at any time by Law make or alter such Regulations, except as to the Places of chusing Senators.

The Congress shall assemble at least once in every Year, and such Meeting shall be on the first Monday in December, unless they shall by Law appoint a different Day.

Section. 5.

Each House shall be the Judge of the Elections, Returns and Qualifications of its own Members, and a Majority of each shall constitute a Quorum to do Business; but a smaller Number may adjourn from day to day, and may be authorized to compel the Attendance of absent Members, in such Manner, and under such Penalties as each House may provide.

Each House may determine the Rules of its Proceedings, punish its Members for disorderly Behaviour, and, with the Concurrence of two thirds, expel a Member.

Each House shall keep a Journal of its Proceedings, and from time to time publish the same, excepting such Parts as may in their Judgment require Secrecy; and the Yeas and Nays of the Members of either House on any question shall, at the Desire of one fifth of those Present, be entered on the Journal.

Neither House, during the Session of Congress, shall, without the Consent of the other, adjourn for more than three days, nor to any other Place than that in which the two Houses shall be sitting.

Section. 6.

The Senators and Representatives shall receive a Compensation for their Services, to be ascertained by Law, and paid out of the Treasury of the United States. They shall in all Cases, except Treason, Felony and Breach of the Peace, be privileged from Arrest during their Attendance at the Session of their respective Houses, and in going to and returning from the

same; and for any Speech or Debate in either House, they shall not be questioned in any other Place.

No Senator or Representative shall, during the Time for which he was elected, be appointed to any civil Office under the Authority of the United States, which shall have been created, or the Emoluments whereof shall have been encreased during such time; and no Person holding any Office under the United States, shall be a Member of either House during his Continuance in Office.

Section. 7.

All Bills for raising Revenue shall originate in the House of Representatives; but the Senate may propose or concur with Amendments as on other Bills.

Every Bill which shall have passed the House of Representatives and the Senate, shall, before it become a Law, be presented to the President of the United States: If he approve he shall sign it, but if not he shall return it, with his Objections to that House in which it shall have originated, who shall enter the Objections at large on their Journal, and proceed to reconsider it. If after such Reconsideration two thirds of that House shall agree to pass the Bill, it shall be sent, together with the Objections, to the other House, by which it shall likewise be reconsidered, and if approved by two thirds of that House, it shall become a Law. But in all such Cases the Votes of both Houses shall be determined by yeas and Nays, and the Names of the Persons voting for and against the Bill shall be entered on the Journal of each House respectively. If any Bill shall not be returned by the President within ten Days (Sundays excepted) after it shall have been presented to him, the Same shall be a Law, in like Manner as if he had signed it, unless the Congress by their Adjournment prevent its Return, in which Case it shall not be a Law.

Every Order, Resolution, or Vote to which the Concurrence of the Senate and House of Representatives may be necessary (except on a question of Adjournment) shall be presented to the President of the United States; and before the Same shall take Effect, shall be approved by him, or being disapproved by him, shall be repassed by two thirds of the Senate and House of Representatives, according to the Rules and Limitations prescribed in the Case of a Bill.

Section. 8.

The Congress shall have Power To lay and collect Taxes, Duties, Imposts and Excises, to pay the Debts and provide for the common Defence and general Welfare of the United States; but all Duties, Imposts and Excises shall be uniform throughout the United States;

To borrow Money on the credit of the United States;

To regulate Commerce with foreign Nations, and among the several States, and with the Indian Tribes;

To establish an uniform Rule of Naturalization, and uniform Laws on the subject of Bankruptcies throughout the United States;

To coin Money, regulate the Value thereof, and of foreign Coin, and fix the Standard of Weights and Measures;

To provide for the Punishment of counterfeiting the Securities and current Coin of the United States;

To establish Post Offices and post Roads;

To promote the Progress of Science and useful Arts, by securing for limited Times to Authors and Inventors the exclusive Right to their respective Writings and Discoveries;

To constitute Tribunals inferior to the supreme Court;

To define and punish Piracies and Felonies committed on the high Seas, and Offences against the Law of Nations;

To declare War, grant Letters of Marque and Reprisal, and make Rules concerning Captures on Land and Water;

To raise and support Armies, but no Appropriation of Money to that Use shall be for a longer Term than two Years;

To provide and maintain a Navy;

To make Rules for the Government and Regulation of the land and naval Forces;

To provide for calling forth the Militia to execute the Laws of the Union, suppress Insurrections and repel Invasions;

To provide for organizing, arming, and disciplining, the Militia, and for governing such Part of them as may be employed in the Service

of the United States, reserving to the States respectively, the Appointment of the Officers, and the Authority of training the Militia according to the discipline prescribed by Congress;

To exercise exclusive Legislation in all Cases whatsoever, over such District (not exceeding ten Miles square) as may, by Cession of particular States, and the Acceptance of Congress, become the Seat of the Government of the United States, and to exercise like Authority over all Places purchased by the Consent of the Legislature of the State in which the Same shall be, for the Erection of Forts, Magazines, Arsenals, dock-Yards, and other needful Buildings;—And

To make all Laws which shall be necessary and proper for carrying into Execution the foregoing Powers, and all other Powers vested by this Constitution in the Government of the United States, or in any Department or Officer thereof.

Section. 9.

The Migration or Importation of such Persons as any of the States now existing shall think proper to admit, shall not be prohibited by the Congress prior to the Year one thousand eight hundred and eight, but a Tax or duty may be imposed on such Importation, not exceeding ten dollars for each Person.

The Privilege of the Writ of Habeas Corpus shall not be suspended, unless when in Cases of Rebellion or Invasion the public Safety may require it.

No Bill of Attainder or ex post facto Law shall be passed.

No Capitation, or other direct, Tax shall be laid, unless in Proportion to the Census or enumeration herein before directed to be taken.

No Tax or Duty shall be laid on Articles exported from any State.

No Preference shall be given by any Regulation of Commerce or Revenue to the Ports of one State over those of another; nor shall Vessels bound to, or from, one State, be obliged to enter, clear, or pay Duties in another.

No Money shall be drawn from the Treasury, but in Consequence of Appropriations made by Law; and a regular Statement and Account of the Receipts and Expenditures of all public Money shall be published from time to time.

No Title of Nobility shall be granted by the United States: And no Person holding any Office of Profit or Trust under them, shall, without the Consent of the Congress, accept of any present, Emolument, Office, or Title, of any kind whatever, from any King, Prince, or foreign State.

Section. 10.

No State shall enter into any Treaty, Alliance, or Confederation; grant Letters of Marque and Reprisal; coin Money; emit Bills of Credit; make any Thing but gold and silver Coin a Tender in Payment of Debts; pass any Bill of Attainder, ex post facto Law, or Law impairing the Obligation of Contracts, or grant any Title of Nobility.

No State shall, without the Consent of the Congress, lay any Imposts or Duties on Imports or Exports, except what may be absolutely necessary for executing it's inspection Laws: and the net Produce of all Duties and Imposts, laid by any State on Imports or Exports, shall be for the Use of the Treasury of the United States; and all such Laws shall be subject to the Revision and Controul of the Congress.

No State shall, without the Consent of Congress, lay any Duty of Tonnage, keep Troops, or Ships of War in time of Peace, enter into any Agreement or Compact with another State, or with a foreign Power, or engage in War, unless actually invaded, or in such imminent Danger as will not admit of delay.

Article. II.

Section. 1.

The executive Power shall be vested in a President of the United States of America. He shall hold his Office during the Term of four Years, and, together with the Vice President, chosen for the same Term, be elected, as follows:

Each State shall appoint, in such Manner as the Legislature thereof may direct, a Number of Electors, equal to the whole Number of Senators and Representatives to which the State may be entitled in the Congress: but no Senator or Representative, or Person holding an Office of Trust or Profit under the United States, shall be appointed an Elector.

The Electors shall meet in their respective States, and vote by Ballot for two Persons, of whom one at least shall not be an Inhabitant of the same State with themselves. And they shall make a List of all the Persons voted for, and of the Number of Votes for each; which List they shall

sign and certify, and transmit sealed to the Seat of the Government of the United States, directed to the President of the Senate. The President of the Senate shall, in the Presence of the Senate and House of Representatives, open all the Certificates, and the Votes shall then be counted. The Person having the greatest Number of Votes shall be the President, if such Number be a Majority of the whole Number of Electors appointed; and if there be more than one who have such Majority, and have an equal Number of Votes, then the House of Representatives shall immediately chuse by Ballot one of them for President; and if no Person have a Majority, then from the five highest on the List the said House shall in like Manner chuse the President. But in chusing the President, the Votes shall be taken by States, the Representation from each State having one Vote; A quorum for this purpose shall consist of a Member or Members from two thirds of the States, and a Majority of all the States shall be necessary to a Choice. In every Case, after the Choice of the President, the Person having the greatest Number of Votes of the Electors shall be the Vice President. But if there should remain two or more who have equal Votes, the Senate shall chuse from them by Ballot the Vice President.

The Congress may determine the Time of chusing the Electors, and the Day on which they shall give their Votes; which Day shall be the same throughout the United States.

No Person except a natural born Citizen, or a Citizen of the United States, at the time of the Adoption of this Constitution, shall be eligible to the Office of President; neither shall any Person be eligible to that Office who shall not have attained to the Age of thirty five Years, and been fourteen Years a Resident within the United States.

In Case of the Removal of the President from Office, or of his Death, Resignation, or Inability to discharge the Powers and Duties of the said Office, the Same shall devolve on the Vice President, and the Congress may by Law provide for the Case of Removal, Death, Resignation or Inability, both of the President and Vice President, declaring what Officer shall then act as President, and such Officer shall act accordingly, until the Disability be removed, or a President shall be elected.

The President shall, at stated Times, receive for his Services, a Compensation, which shall neither be increased nor diminished during the Period for which he shall have been elected, and he shall not receive within that Period any other Emolument from the United States, or any of them.

Before he enter on the Execution of his Office, he shall take the following Oath or Affirmation:—"I do solemnly swear (or affirm) that I will faithfully execute the Office of President of the United States, and will to the best of my Ability, preserve, protect and defend the Constitution of the United States."

Section. 2.

The President shall be Commander in Chief of the Army and Navy of the United States, and of the Militia of the several States, when called into the actual Service of the United States; he may require the Opinion, in writing, of the principal Officer in each of the executive Departments, upon any Subject relating to the Duties of their respective Offices, and he shall have Power to grant Reprieves and Pardons for Offences against the United States, except in Cases of Impeachment.

He shall have Power, by and with the Advice and Consent of the Senate, to make Treaties, provided two thirds of the Senators present concur; and he shall nominate, and by and with the Advice and Consent of the Senate, shall appoint Ambassadors, other public Ministers and Consuls, Judges of the supreme Court, and all other Officers of the United States, whose Appointments are not herein otherwise provided for, and which shall be established by Law: but the Congress may by Law vest the Appointment of such inferior Officers, as they think proper, in the President alone, in the Courts of Law, or in the Heads of Departments.

The President shall have Power to fill up all Vacancies that may happen during the Recess of the Senate, by granting Commissions which shall expire at the End of their next Session.

Section. 3.

He shall from time to time give to the Congress Information of the State of the Union, and recommend to their Consideration such Measures as he shall judge necessary and expedient; he may, on extraordinary Occasions, convene both Houses, or either of them, and in Case of Disagreement between them, with Respect to the Time of Adjournment, he may adjourn them to such Time as he shall think proper; he shall receive Ambassadors and other public Ministers; he shall take Care that the Laws be faithfully executed, and shall Commission all the Officers of the United States.

Section. 4.

The President, Vice President and all civil Officers of the United States, shall be removed from Office on Impeachment for, and Conviction of, Treason, Bribery, or other high Crimes and Misdemeanors.

Article. III.

Section. 1.

The judicial Power of the United States shall be vested in one supreme Court, and in such inferior Courts as the Congress may from time to time ordain and establish. The Judges, both of the supreme and inferior Courts, shall hold their Offices during good Behaviour, and shall, at stated Times, receive for their Services a Compensation, which shall not be diminished during their Continuance in Office.

Section. 2.

The judicial Power shall extend to all Cases, in Law and Equity, arising under this Constitution, the Laws of the United States, and Treaties made, or which shall be made, under their Authority;—to all Cases affecting Ambassadors, other public Ministers and Consuls;—to all Cases of admiralty and maritime Jurisdiction;—to Controversies to which the United States shall be a Party;—to Controversies between two or more States;—between a State and Citizens of another State,—between Citizens of different States,—between Citizens of the same State claiming Lands under Grants of different States, and between a State, or the Citizens thereof, and foreign States, Citizens or Subjects.

In all Cases affecting Ambassadors, other public Ministers and Consuls, and those in which a State shall be Party, the supreme Court shall have original Jurisdiction. In all the other Cases before mentioned, the supreme Court shall have appellate Jurisdiction, both as to Law and Fact, with such Exceptions, and under such Regulations as the Congress shall make.

The Trial of all Crimes, except in Cases of Impeachment, shall be by Jury; and such Trial shall be held in the State where the said Crimes shall have been committed; but when not committed within any State, the Trial shall be at such Place or Places as the Congress may by Law have directed.

Section. 3.

Treason against the United States, shall consist only in levying War against them, or in adhering to their Enemies, giving them Aid and Comfort. No Person shall be convicted of Treason unless on the Testimony of two Witnesses to the same overt Act, or on Confession in open Court.

The Congress shall have Power to declare the Punishment of Treason, but no Attainder of Treason shall work Corruption of Blood, or Forfeiture except during the Life of the Person attainted.

Article. IV.

Section. 1.

Full Faith and Credit shall be given in each State to the public Acts, Records, and judicial Proceedings of every other State. And the Congress may by general Laws prescribe the Manner in which such Acts, Records and Proceedings shall be proved, and the Effect thereof.

Section. 2.

The Citizens of each State shall be entitled to all Privileges and Immunities of Citizens in the several States.

A Person charged in any State with Treason, Felony, or other Crime, who shall flee from Justice, and be found in another State, shall on Demand of the executive Authority of the State from which he fled, be delivered up, to be removed to the State having Jurisdiction of the Crime.

No Person held to Service or Labour in one State, under the Laws thereof, escaping into another, shall, in Consequence of any Law or Regulation therein, be discharged from such Service or Labour, but shall be delivered up on Claim of the Party to whom such Service or Labour may be due.

Section. 3.

New States may be admitted by the Congress into this Union; but no new State shall be formed or erected within the Jurisdiction of any other State; nor any State be formed by the Junction of two or more States, or Parts of States, without the Consent of the Legislatures of the States concerned as well as of the Congress.

The Congress shall have Power to dispose of and make all needful Rules and Regulations respecting the Territory or other Property belonging to the United States; and nothing in this Constitution shall be

so construed as to Prejudice any Claims of the United States, or of any particular State.

Section. 4.

The United States shall guarantee to every State in this Union a Republican Form of Government, and shall protect each of them against Invasion; and on Application of the Legislature, or of the Executive (when the Legislature cannot be convened), against domestic Violence.

Article. V.

The Congress, whenever two thirds of both Houses shall deem it necessary, shall propose Amendments to this Constitution, or, on the Application of the Legislatures of two thirds of the several States, shall call a Convention for proposing Amendments, which, in either Case, shall be valid to all Intents and Purposes, as Part of this Constitution, when ratified by the Legislatures of three fourths of the several States, or by Conventions in three fourths thereof, as the one or the other Mode of Ratification may be proposed by the Congress; Provided that no Amendment which may be made prior to the Year One thousand eight hundred and eight shall in any Manner affect the first and fourth Clauses in the Ninth Section of the first Article; and that no State, without its Consent, shall be deprived of its equal Suffrage in the Senate.

Article. VI.

All Debts contracted and Engagements entered into, before the Adoption of this Constitution, shall be as valid against the United States under this Constitution, as under the Confederation.

This Constitution, and the Laws of the United States which shall be made in Pursuance thereof; and all Treaties made, or which shall be made, under the Authority of the United States, shall be the supreme Law of the Land; and the Judges in every State shall be bound thereby, any Thing in the Constitution or Laws of any State to the Contrary notwithstanding.

The Senators and Representatives before mentioned, and the Members of the several State Legislatures, and all executive and judicial Officers, both of the United States and of the several States, shall be bound by Oath or Affirmation, to support this Constitution; but no religious Test shall ever be required as a Qualification to any Office or public Trust under the United States.

Article. VII.

The Ratification of the Conventions of nine States, shall be sufficient for the Establishment of this Constitution between the States so ratifying the Same.

The Word, "the," being interlined between the seventh and eighth Lines of the first Page, the Word "Thirty" being partly written on an Erazure in the fifteenth Line of the first Page, The Words "is tried" being interlined between the thirty second and thirty third Lines of the first Page and the Word "the" being interlined between the forty third and forty fourth Lines of the second Page.

Attest William Jackson Secretary

done in Convention by the Unanimous Consent of the States present the Seventeenth Day of September in the Year of our Lord one thousand seven hundred and Eighty seven and of the Independance of the United States of America the Twelfth In witness whereof We have hereunto subscribed our Names,

---

G°. Washington
*Presidt and deputy
from Virginia*

Delaware
*Geo: Read
Gunning Bedford jun
John Dickinson
Richard Bassett
Jaco: Broom*

Maryland
*James McHenry
Dan of St Thos. Jenifer
Danl. Carroll*

Virginia
*John Blair
James Madison Jr.*

North Carolina
*Wm. Blount
Richd. Dobbs Spaight
Hu Williamson*

South Carolina
*J. Rutledge
Charles Cotesworth
Pinckney
Charles Pinckney
Pierce Butler*

Georgia
*William Few
Abr Baldwin*

New Hampshire
*John Langdon
Nicholas Gilman*

Massachusetts
*Nathaniel Gorham
Rufus King*

Connecticut
*Wm. Saml. Johnson
Roger Sherman*

New York
Alexander Hamilton

New Jersey
*Wil: Livingston
David Brearley
Wm. Paterson
Jona: Dayton*

Pennsylvania
*B Franklin
Thomas Mifflin
Robt. Morris
Geo. Clymer
Thos. FitzSimons
Jared Ingersoll
James Wilson
Gouv Morris*

The Bill of Rights

The Preamble to The Bill of Rights

Congress of the United States
*begun and held at the City of New-York,
on Wednesday the fourth of March,
one thousand seven hundred and eighty nine.*

THE Conventions of a number of the States, having at the time of their adopting the Constitution, expressed a desire, in order to prevent misconstruction or abuse of its powers, that further declaratory and restrictive clauses should be added: And as extending the ground of public confidence in the Government, will best ensure the beneficent ends of its institution.

RESOLVED by the Senate and House of Representatives of the United States of America, in Congress assembled, two thirds of both Houses concurring, that the following Articles be proposed to the Legislatures of the several States, as amendments to the Constitution of the United States, all, or any of which Articles, when ratified by three fourths of the said Legislatures, to be valid to all intents and purposes, as part of the said Constitution; viz.

ARTICLES in addition to, and Amendment of the Constitution of the United States of America, proposed by Congress, and ratified by the Legislatures of the several States, pursuant to the fifth Article of the original Constitution.

Note: *The following text is a transcription of the first ten amendments to the Constitution in their original form. These amendments were ratified December 15, 1791, and form what is known as the "Bill of Rights."*

Amendment I
Congress shall make no law respecting an establishment of religion, or prohibiting the free exercise thereof; or abridging the freedom of speech,

or of the press; or the right of the people peaceably to assemble, and to petition the Government for a redress of grievances.

Amendment II

A well regulated Militia, being necessary to the security of a free State, the right of the people to keep and bear Arms, shall not be infringed.

Amendment III

No Soldier shall, in time of peace be quartered in any house, without the consent of the Owner, nor in time of war, but in a manner to be prescribed by law.

Amendment IV

The right of the people to be secure in their persons, houses, papers, and effects, against unreasonable searches and seizures, shall not be violated, and no Warrants shall issue, but upon probable cause, supported by Oath or affirmation, and particularly describing the place to be searched, and the persons or things to be seized.

Amendment V

No person shall be held to answer for a capital, or otherwise infamous crime, unless on a presentment or indictment of a Grand Jury, except in cases arising in the land or naval forces, or in the Militia, when in actual service in time of War or public danger; nor shall any person be subject for the same offence to be twice put in jeopardy of life or limb; nor shall be compelled in any criminal case to be a witness against himself, nor be deprived of life, liberty, or property, without due process of law; nor shall private property be taken for public use, without just compensation.

Amendment VI

In all criminal prosecutions, the accused shall enjoy the right to a speedy and public trial, by an impartial jury of the State and district wherein the crime shall have been committed, which district shall have been previously ascertained by law, and to be informed of the nature and cause of the accusation; to be confronted with the witnesses against him; to have compulsory process for obtaining witnesses in his favor, and to have the Assistance of Counsel for his defence.

Amendment VII

In Suits at common law, where the value in controversy shall exceed twenty dollars, the right of trial by jury shall be preserved, and no fact tried by a jury, shall be otherwise re-examined in any Court of the United States, than according to the rules of the common law.

Amendment VIII

Excessive bail shall not be required, nor excessive fines imposed, nor cruel and unusual punishments inflicted.

Amendment IX

The enumeration in the Constitution, of certain rights, shall not be construed to deny or disparage others retained by the people.

Amendment X

The powers not delegated to the United States by the Constitution, nor prohibited by it to the States, are reserved to the States respectively, or to the people.

Amendments XI–XXVII

Amendment XI

Passed by Congress March 4, 1794.
Ratified February 7, 1795.
Note: Article III, section 2, of the Constitution
was modified by amendment 11.

The Judicial power of the United States shall not be construed to extend to any suit in law or equity, commenced or prosecuted against one of the United States by Citizens of another State, or by Citizens or Subjects of any Foreign State.

Amendment XII

Passed by Congress December 9, 1803.
Ratified June 15, 1804.
Note: A portion of Article II, section 1 of the
Constitution was superseded by the 12th amendment.

The Electors shall meet in their respective states and vote by ballot for President and Vice-President, one of whom, at least, shall not be an inhabitant of the same state with themselves; they shall name in their ballots the person voted for as President, and in distinct ballots the person voted for as Vice-President, and they shall make distinct lists of all persons voted for as President, and of all persons voted for as Vice-President, and of the number of votes for each, which lists they shall sign and certify, and transmit sealed to the seat of the government of the United States, directed to the President of the Senate; —the President of the Senate shall, in the presence of the Senate and House of Representatives, open all the certificates and the votes shall then be counted; —The person having the greatest number of votes for President, shall be the President, if such number be a majority of the whole number of Electors appointed; and if no person have such majority, then from the persons having the highest numbers not exceeding three on the list of those voted for as President, the House of Representatives shall choose immediately, by ballot, the President. But in choosing the President, the votes shall be taken by states, the representation from each state having one vote; a quorum for this purpose shall consist of a member or members from two-

thirds of the states, and a majority of all the states shall be necessary to a choice. [And if the House of Representatives shall not choose a President whenever the right of choice shall devolve upon them, before the fourth day of March next following, then the Vice-President shall act as President, as in case of the death or other constitutional disability of the President. —]* The person having the greatest number of votes as Vice-President, shall be the Vice-President, if such number be a majority of the whole number of Electors appointed, and if no person have a majority, then from the two highest numbers on the list, the Senate shall choose the Vice-President; a quorum for the purpose shall consist of two-thirds of the whole number of Senators, and a majority of the whole number shall be necessary to a choice. But no person constitutionally ineligible to the office of President shall be eligible to that of Vice-President of the United States.

Superseded by section 3 of the 20th amendment.

Amendment XIII

Passed by Congress January 31, 1865.
Ratified December 6, 1865.

Note: A portion of Article IV, section 2, of the Constitution was superseded by the 13th amendment.

Section 1.

Neither slavery nor involuntary servitude, except as a punishment for crime whereof the party shall have been duly convicted, shall exist within the United States, or any place subject to their jurisdiction.

Section 2.

Congress shall have power to enforce this article by appropriate legislation.

Amendment XIV

Passed by Congress June 13, 1866.
Ratified July 9, 1868.

Note: Article I, section 2, of the Constitution was modified by section 2 of the 14th amendment.

Section 1.

All persons born or naturalized in the United States, and subject to the jurisdiction thereof, are citizens of the United States and of the State wherein they reside. No State shall make or enforce any law which shall abridge the privileges or immunities of citizens of the United States; nor shall any State deprive any person of life, liberty, or property, without due process of law; nor deny to any person within its jurisdiction the equal protection of the laws.

Section 2.

Representatives shall be apportioned among the several States according to their respective numbers, counting the whole number of persons in each State, excluding Indians not taxed. But when the right to vote at any election for the choice of electors for President and Vice-President of the United States, Representatives in Congress, the Executive and Judicial officers of a State, or the members of the Legislature thereof, is denied to any of the male inhabitants of such State, being twenty-one years of age,* and citizens of the United States, or in any way abridged, except for participation in rebellion, or other crime, the basis of representation therein shall be reduced in the proportion which the number of such male citizens shall bear to the whole number of male citizens twenty-one years of age in such State.

Section 3.

No person shall be a Senator or Representative in Congress, or elector of President and Vice-President, or hold any office, civil or military, under the United States, or under any State, who, having previously taken an oath, as a member of Congress, or as an officer of the United States, or as a member of any State legislature, or as an executive or judicial officer of any State, to support the Constitution of the United States, shall have engaged in insurrection or rebellion against the same, or given aid or comfort to the enemies thereof. But Congress may by a vote of two-thirds of each House, remove such disability.

Section 4.

The validity of the public debt of the United States, authorized by law, including debts incurred for payment of pensions and bounties for services in suppressing insurrection or rebellion, shall not be questioned. But neither the United States nor any State shall assume or pay any debt or obligation incurred in aid of insurrection or rebellion against the United States, or any claim for the loss or emancipation of any slave; but all such debts, obligations and claims shall be held illegal and void.

Section 5.

The Congress shall have the power to enforce, by appropriate legislation, the provisions of this article.

*Changed by section 1 of the 26th amendment.

Amendment XV

Passed by Congress February 26, 1869.
Ratified February 3, 1870.

Section 1.

The right of citizens of the United States to vote shall not be denied or abridged by the United States or by any State on account of race, color, or previous condition of servitude—

Section 2.

The Congress shall have the power to enforce this article by appropriate legislation.

Amendment XVI

Passed by Congress July 2, 1909.
Ratified February 3, 1913.
Note: Article I, section 9, of the Constitution
was modified by amendment 16.

The Congress shall have power to lay and collect taxes on incomes, from whatever source derived, without apportionment among the several States, and without regard to any census or enumeration.

Amendment XVII

Passed by Congress May 13, 1912.
Ratified April 8, 1913.
Note: Article I, section 3, of the Constitution
was modified by the 17th amendment.

The Senate of the United States shall be composed of two Senators from each State, elected by the people thereof, for six years; and each Senator shall have one vote. The electors in each State shall have the qualifications requisite for electors of the most numerous branch of the State legislatures.

When vacancies happen in the representation of any State in the Senate, the executive authority of such State shall issue writs of election to fill such vacancies: Provided, That the legislature of any State may empower the executive thereof to make temporary appointments until the people fill the vacancies by election as the legislature may direct.

This amendment shall not be so construed as to affect the election or term of any Senator chosen before it becomes valid as part of the Constitution.

Amendment XVIII

Passed by Congress December 18, 1917.
Ratified January 16, 1919.
Repealed by amendment 21.

Section 1.

After one year from the ratification of this article the manufacture, sale, or transportation of intoxicating liquors within, the importation thereof into, or the exportation thereof from the United States and all territory subject to the jurisdiction thereof for beverage purposes is hereby prohibited.

Section 2.

The Congress and the several States shall have concurrent power to enforce this article by appropriate legislation.

Section 3.

This article shall be inoperative unless it shall have been ratified as an amendment to the Constitution by the legislatures of the several States, as provided in the Constitution, within seven years from the date of the submission hereof to the States by the Congress.

Amendment XIX

Passed by Congress June 4, 1919.
Ratified August 18, 1920.

The right of citizens of the United States to vote shall not be denied or abridged by the United States or by any State on account of sex.

Congress shall have power to enforce this article by appropriate legislation.

Amendment XX

Passed by Congress March 2, 1932.
Ratified January 23, 1933.
Note: Article I, section 4, of the Constitution
was modified by section 2 of this amendment. In addition,
a portion of the 12th amendment was superseded by section 3.

Section 1.

The terms of the President and the Vice President shall end at noon on the 20th day of January, and the terms of Senators and Representatives at noon on the 3d day of January, of the years in which such terms would have ended if this article had not been ratified; and the terms of their successors shall then begin.

Section 2.

The Congress shall assemble at least once in every year, and such meeting shall begin at noon on the 3d day of January, unless they shall by law appoint a different day.

Section 3.

If, at the time fixed for the beginning of the term of the President, the President elect shall have died, the Vice President elect shall become President. If a President shall not have been chosen before the time fixed for the beginning of his term, or if the President elect shall have failed to qualify, then the Vice President elect shall act as President until a President shall have qualified; and the Congress may by law provide for the case wherein neither a President elect nor a Vice President shall have qualified, declaring who shall then act as President, or the manner in which one who is to act shall be selected, and such person shall act accordingly until a President or Vice President shall have qualified.

Section 4.

The Congress may by law provide for the case of the death of any of the persons from whom the House of Representatives may choose a President whenever the right of choice shall have devolved upon them, and for the case of the death of any of the persons from whom the Senate may choose a Vice President whenever the right of choice shall have devolved upon them.

Section 5.
Sections 1 and 2 shall take effect on the 15th day of October following the ratification of this article.

Section 6.
This article shall be inoperative unless it shall have been ratified as an amendment to the Constitution by the legislatures of three-fourths of the several States within seven years from the date of its submission.

Amendment XXI

Passed by Congress February 20, 1933.
Ratified December 5, 1933.

Section 1.
The eighteenth article of amendment to the Constitution of the United States is hereby repealed.

Section 2.
The transportation or importation into any State, Territory, or Possession of the United States for delivery or use therein of intoxicating liquors, in violation of the laws thereof, is hereby prohibited.

Section 3.
This article shall be inoperative unless it shall have been ratified as an amendment to the Constitution by conventions in the several States, as provided in the Constitution, within seven years from the date of the submission hereof to the States by the Congress.

Amendment XXII

Passed by Congress March 21, 1947.
Ratified February 27, 1951.

Section 1.
No person shall be elected to the office of the President more than twice, and no person who has held the office of President, or acted as President, for more than two years of a term to which some other person was elected President shall be elected to the office of President more than once. But this Article shall not apply to any person holding the office of President when this Article was proposed by Congress, and shall not prevent any person who may be holding the office of President, or acting as

President, during the term within which this Article becomes operative from holding the office of President or acting as President during the remainder of such term.

Section 2.

This article shall be inoperative unless it shall have been ratified as an amendment to the Constitution by the legislatures of three-fourths of the several States within seven years from the date of its submission to the States by the Congress.

Amendment XXIII

Passed by Congress June 16, 1960.
Ratified March 29, 1961.

Section 1.

The District constituting the seat of Government of the United States shall appoint in such manner as Congress may direct:

A number of electors of President and Vice President equal to the whole number of Senators and Representatives in Congress to which the District would be entitled if it were a State, but in no event more than the least populous State; they shall be in addition to those appointed by the States, but they shall be considered, for the purposes of the election of President and Vice President, to be electors appointed by a State; and they shall meet in the District and perform such duties as provided by the twelfth article of amendment.

Section 2.

The Congress shall have power to enforce this article by appropriate legislation.

Amendment XXIV

Passed by Congress August 27, 1962.
Ratified January 23, 1964.

Section 1.

The right of citizens of the United States to vote in any primary or other election for President or Vice President, for electors for President or Vice President, or for Senator or Representative in Congress, shall not be denied or abridged by the United States or any State by reason of failure to pay poll tax or other tax.

Section 2.

The Congress shall have power to enforce this article by appropriate legislation.

Amendment XXV

Passed by Congress July 6, 1965.
Ratified February 10, 1967.
Note: Article II, section 1, of the Constitution
was affected by the 25th amendment.

Section 1.

In case of the removal of the President from office or of his death or resignation, the Vice President shall become President.

Section 2.

Whenever there is a vacancy in the office of the Vice President, the President shall nominate a Vice President who shall take office upon confirmation by a majority vote of both Houses of Congress.

Section 3.

Whenever the President transmits to the President pro tempore of the Senate and the Speaker of the House of Representatives his written declaration that he is unable to discharge the powers and duties of his office, and until he transmits to them a written declaration to the contrary, such powers and duties shall be discharged by the Vice President as Acting President.

Section 4.

Whenever the Vice President and a majority of either the principal officers of the executive departments or of such other body as Congress may by law provide, transmit to the President pro tempore of the Senate and the Speaker of the House of Representatives their written declaration that the President is unable to discharge the powers and duties of his office, the Vice President shall immediately assume the powers and duties of the office as Acting President.

Thereafter, when the President transmits to the President pro tempore of the Senate and the Speaker of the House of Representatives his written declaration that no inability exists, he shall resume the powers and duties of his office unless the Vice President and a majority of either

the principal officers of the executive department or of such other body as Congress may by law provide, transmit within four days to the President pro tempore of the Senate and the Speaker of the House of Representatives their written declaration that the President is unable to discharge the powers and duties of his office. Thereupon Congress shall decide the issue, assembling within forty-eight hours for that purpose if not in session. If the Congress, within twenty-one days after receipt of the latter written declaration, or, if Congress is not in session, within twenty-one days after Congress is required to assemble, determines by two-thirds vote of both Houses that the President is unable to discharge the powers and duties of his office, the Vice President shall continue to discharge the same as Acting President; otherwise, the President shall resume the powers and duties of his office.

Amendment XXVI

Passed by Congress March 23, 1971.
Ratified July 1, 1971.
Note: Amendment 14, section 2, of the Constitution
was modified by section 1 of the 26th amendment.

Section 1.

The right of citizens of the United States, who are eighteen years of age or older, to vote shall not be denied or abridged by the United States or by any State on account of age.

Section 2.

The Congress shall have power to enforce this article by appropriate legislation.

Amendment XXVII

Originally proposed Sept. 25, 1789.
Ratified May 7, 1992.

No law, varying the compensation for the services of the Senators and Representatives, shall take effect, until an election of representatives shall have intervened.

Index

A

Accomplishments, credit for, 43–45, 59

Adams, Douglas, 103

Adams, Henry, 31

Adams, Samuel, 81

Adjournment date, 62

Agenda of party, 45, 82

Ambrose, St., 1

Amendments to bills, 36–37, 38n3, 38n5

Amendments to Constitution, reprinted, 134–146

Appropriations Committee, 104

Arouet, Francois Marie, 99

B

Baucus, Max, 77, 78, 79

Bierce, Ambrose, 93

Bill of Rights, reprinted, 134–136

Bills. *See* Amendments to bills; Legislation

Blowout Prevention Act of 2010, 48

Boehner, John, 79

Bonus system, 69

"Boss" Tweed, 35

Brandeis, Louis, 63

"Bridge to Nowhere," 45

British Petroleum (BP) oil spill, 48

Brown, Rita Mae, 93

Brown, Scott, 36

Bryson, Lyman, 25

Bubble of congressional life, 31–33, 58, 67–69

Buckley, James L., 39

Budget of each chamber, reduction of, 69

Budget process, 103–107

Burke, Edmund, 63

Bush, George H.W., 33

C

Campaign finance law, 16–17, 19n7, 24n3, 63, 65

Campaign fundraising, 2, 7–8, 63–66

    incumbents and, 15–16, 63, 64, 72

    Internet disclosure of, 65–66

    law on. *See* Campaign finance law

    limits, 16–17, 19n7, 64

    networking and, 26

    prohibiting while Congress in session, 72

    stress of, 22, 26

Campaigning, 21–24

    against incumbent, 21

    minority party, 21–22

    stresses of, 22–24, 27–28

Chekhov, Anton, 47

Cloture, 38n2

Commemorative bills, 41, 74

Commission on entitlement reform, 52–53